REACHING
TRUE
PEACE

Gail –
hey! Thanks so much for extending trust ... warmth ... support.

REACHING
TRUE
PEACE

May your journey unfold with beauty.

7 UNIVERSAL REALMS OF SPIRITUAL DEVELOPMENT

Rod Davis, Ph.D.

Rod Davis

Copyright © 2005 Rod Davis

Fern Haven Press
P.O. Box 2752
Olympia, WA 98507-2752

All rights reserved. No part of this book may be reproduced or used in any form or by any means, electronic or mechanical, including photocopying, recording, or by any information storage or retrieval system, without permission in writing from the Publishers. Inquiries should be addressed to Rod Davis

Publisher's Cataloging-in-Publication
(Provided by Quality Books, Inc.)

Davis, Rod (Rod F.), 1948-
    Reaching true peace : 7 universal realms of spiritual development / Rod Davis.
    p. cm.
    Includes bibliographical references and index.
    ISBN: 0-9754078-0-5

    1. Spirituality--Psychology. 2. Kundalini.
3. Teresa of Avila, Saint, 1515-1582. 4. Jung, C. G. (Carl Gustav), 1875-1961. I. Title.

BL624.D38 2005   200'.1'9
                          QBI04-700289

Project Management: Sylvia Hemmerly
Interior Design & Typesetting: Publishing Professionals
Cover Design: Debi Bodett, 33 Image Design

Printed in Canada

Dedication

"To that deep hidden fire that burns within each of us. . .

    which, in the end, becomes the radiance of true peace"

Table of Contents

Introduction 1

Chapter 1 The Psychology of Spiritual
          Development 5

Chapter 2 The Symbolism of Kundalini Yoga 15

Chapter 3 Many Dwelling Places in the Castle
          of the Psyche 33

Chapter 4 Meditation and the Integration
          of the Psyche 53

Chapter 5 First Realm: The Call to Awakening 71

Chapter 6 Second Realm: The Battlefield of
          the Personal Unconscious 97

Chapter 7 Third Realm: The Fire Sacrifice 121

Chapter 8 Fourth Realm: Birth of the
          Spiritual Self 141

Chapter 9 Fifth Realm: Deconstructing
          the Mind-process 161

Chapter 10 The Sixth Realm: The Empyreal
          Heaven Within Ourselves 179

Chapter 11 The Seventh Realm: The 'Peace that
          Passeth All Understanding' 197

Chapter 12 Conclusion: Walking on Our Path 215

End Notes 221

Bibliography 225

Glossary 227

Index 231

Introduction

Spiritual development is a journey in consciousness, and this book is a map and guidebook for the spiritual explorer. It draws on two authentic spiritual traditions, one Eastern and one Western, that provide, each in its own unique way, a map and description of the wild and unexplored territory that we who desire to undertake this journey must traverse. These are the chakra system as embedded in the kundalini yoga tradition, and the well-known text, *Interior Castle*, written by sixteenth-century Spanish Christian mystic, Teresa of Avila. Both of these paint a picture of seven realms within the interior depths of our being, and seven corresponding stages of spiritual development. They are different maps of the same territory.

Kundalini yoga is presented to us as a symbolic system that is difficult to understand, even for those with some background in the yoga tradition. *Interior Castle* is somewhat more accessible, but also utilizes images, analogies, and religious language that require careful interpretation. In taking a close look at these two 'maps' of human consciousness and unfolding their vision of spiritual development, we will be using a language and framework provided by the modern Western discipline of depth psychology, particularly the work of famous Swiss psychologist, Carl Jung.

Depth psychology, with its focus on the dynamic relationship of conscious and unconscious within our being, is particularly well suited to exploring and unfolding the meaning of these two spiritual systems. Both envision the human psyche in its universal 'depth' dimension. And both also present possibilities for the development of consciousness that even Jung could not accept. By using the 'lens' of depth psychology to look deeper and venture farther than is normally done, we will find that it provides a clear 'language' that we can use to understand the nature of spiritual development. The light of that new understanding and insight is very relevant to our modern life and culture. It can help illumine the unique path that each of us treads as we seek to fulfill our destiny.

So we are building a coherent spiritual psychology, drawing on the three streams of kundalini yoga, *Interior Castle*, and depth psychology. It is a creative and exciting exploration, and a truly 'integral' work. It is grounded both on universal principles of spiritual development and on the actual psychological processes by which spiritual travelers like you and me can radically transform ourselves from within. As such, it makes a unique, genuine, and important contribution to the whole field of psychology and spirituality. Its strength lay in its synthesis of authentic Eastern and Western spiritual systems with our modern understanding of the dynamic nature of the human psyche.

Only occasionally do I discuss my own experience when it can shed some light on a particular aspect of this journey of deep transformation and integration. I am a long-time student of the yoga tradition and have been walking on my path of development for some time. A desire to integrate my vital inner life and my not-so-vital outer 'work' life led me some years ago to a Ph.D. program in East-West Psychology. That gave me a solid grounding in depth psychology as well as in certain Western spiritual traditions that focus on each person's potential for true peace.

Each of us, of course, have the responsibility to develop our own vision of our journey in life so that we can walk forward confidently on our path. This book can provide much food for thought in that regard. It suggests and lays out a path to the deepest possible integration and unification of our being, and to the 'peace that passeth all understanding'. It looks in some detail at the various stages of this journey, the many challenges that we will meet, and the nature of the territory that we will pass through.

No journey, no adventure is as thrilling or as challenging as real spiritual development. The inner call to develop and realize the deeper potentials latent within our consciousness comes to all of us at some point. Our task is to find our path and learn to walk on it to the best of our ability. Then, even if, at times, we cannot see the way, it will open before us just enough to keep us moving forward.

I hope you enjoy reading the book as I have enjoyed writing it. Take time to contemplate the journey it describes. And above all, keep walking on your path until all the hidden potentials within you have come forth into the full light of day.

Chapter 1

The Psychology of Spiritual Development

"Everything in the unconscious seeks outward manifestation, and the personality too desires to evolve out of its unconscious conditions and to experience itself as a whole."
          CARL JUNG, IN *Memories, Dreams, Reflections*[1]

TWO SEVEN-STAGE SYSTEMS OF SPIRITUAL DEVELOPMENT

Though far apart in culture and history, both *Interior Castle* and kundalini yoga can be understood as symbolic systems of spiritual development, and both present a similar vision of the general stages of transformation and transcendence. *Interior Castle*, written in 1577, is an account of seven stages in the aspiring individual's journey toward 'union with God'. Long recognized as one of the masterpieces of Christian mysticism, it was written by Teresa of Avila (1515–1582), a Spanish Carmelite nun who founded a new order—the Discalced Carmelites—that focused on the cultivation of spiritual realization while living a life of simplicity, renunciation, and service. Teresa wrote it for the benefit of the 'sisters' within her order, but not only for them, for all sincere spiritual seekers. Although her language reflects her own tradition and culture, her essential message is universal and timeless. It is as 'alive' today as the day it was written.

Kundalini yoga, on the other hand, is a collective expression of many sages and yogis, developed over hundreds, if not thousands of years, and anonymously embedded in the vast world of Indian spirituality. The heart of this tradition is the chakra system, a series of seven spiritual centers aligned along the spinal column of the human body, from the base of the spine to the crown of the head. The Sanskrit word *chakra* is most often translated in English as 'wheel' or 'disc'. Each chakra is represented by its own circular, mandala-based symbolism.

The chakra system has gained some visibility and popularity in the West in recent years, and is now widely regarded for its universal appeal and applicability as a map of psychological and spiritual transformation. It is, however, difficult to understand just what the abstract visual symbolism of the chakras is all about. My long training and practice within the yoga tradition has given me the confidence to approach this system with respect and care in unfolding its essential significance. As a self-contained symbolic system of spiritual development, it has few equals. The power of its vision is also deep, universal, and timeless.

☙

A PATH TO 'COMPLETE CONSCIOUSNESS'

The seven-stage approach that kundalini yoga and *Interior Castle* share provides a simple internal structure and organization to what might otherwise seem like a complex web of transformational processes that are difficult to envision in their overall pattern and totality. The seven chakras and the seven 'dwelling places' of the 'interior castle' that is our being, present a system of development that characterizes the dynamic transformation of individual consciousness through every major phase in the awakening of our full spiritual potential. They present a picture of the progressive integration of our being at deeper and deeper levels until, finally, our whole being, from the surface of our awareness to the deepest core of the unconscious, is completely unified and illumined. All unconsciousness disappears, and we dwell in complete clarity and peace.

Spiritual realization can be understood as a process of 'waking up' or becoming conscious in the depths of the unconscious.[2] It is, of course, impossible for us to imagine this wholeness or 'complete consciousness' in which all unconscious forces and tendencies are rendered powerless. Never again would we be the victim of fear, worry, anxiety, anger, or any other unwanted feeling. Not even the death of the body could evoke fear in us. Never again would we experience that inescapable sense of separateness and limitation that characterizes our personal life. The duality of 'I' and 'other' or 'world' would be dissolved in the realization of Unity.

JUNG AND KUNDALINI YOGA

In utilizing the seven-stage framework that is provided by *Interior Castle* and the chakra system, I unfold their meaning and significance as 'realms' of spiritual development with two objects in mind: first, to be true to them, as given by the author in the case of *Interior Castle*, and as given by the tradition in which it is embedded in the case of kundalini yoga. Second, to translate them into the language of depth psychology, in which the polarity of conscious and unconscious and the dynamic relationship between these two poles of our being is paramount.

The famous Swiss psychologist, Carl Jung (1875–1961), was a true explorer of the human psyche and a pioneer of depth psychology. He developed his own understanding of psychological and spiritual development and used the term 'individuation' to describe this process. In 1932 he held a series of four seminars in Zurich on the subject of kundalini yoga. The transcripts of these seminars were not publicly available until 1996 when *The Psychology of Kundalini Yoga* was published.

Jung's comments on the chakra system as a developmental model, and its relationship to his own understanding of individuation, constitute an important resource for the discussion that follows. His insights are powerful, even though some of his conclusions may not be consistent with the yoga tradition. He realized that the lowest chakra represents the normal waking state of human consciousness, and that the higher chakras symbolize progressively deeper levels of the personal and universal unconscious. Jung's lectures, although limited and deficient in many respects, represent a vital early link between depth psychology and the tradition of kundalini yoga.

WHOLENESS AND INDIVIDUATION

In the world of depth psychology, the term 'wholeness' is used to imply a state in which our conscious mind has opened itself and built a bridge to the mystery and depth and wisdom of the deep unconscious. It is a relative state of integration between our individual consciousness and the vastness of the unconscious. As we grow whole, we deepen our personality, infusing it with a rich source of creative energy and bringing it into dynamic relationship with the universal, spiritual, 'eternal' forces of the collective human psyche.

Jung envisioned the journey of 'individuation' as becoming a more whole, more integrated, more fully conscious individual. That this process is essentially spiritual in nature was obvious to him. Cast by some of his followers as almost a modern day prophet, he calls us back to the revitalization of our inner life, which has suffered so sorely in the modern quest for material advancement. He knew firsthand that religion, for so many people, has lost its power of connection with the depths of consciousness. So he forged a psychology of individual development that promised access to those depths and the rewards of a spiritually enriched consciousness. That his work found fertile ground in which to grow hardly needs to be said. His influence on the collective modern consciousness is immense.

Indeed, Jung saw clearly the psychological dilemma of modern man. Fascinated by the sense of our own power to manipulate nature, but increasingly estranged from our psychological and spiritual roots, we are subject to the tyranny of potent unconscious forces hidden behind the surface of our 'externalized' consciousness. His thorough and convincing documentation of the reality of our 'psyche', in all its unknown interior depth, is one of the modern world's most cogent statements for the great need we humans have for a vital inner life, for the psychological and spiritual development of our consciousness.

As revolutionary and timely as his message was and 'is', Jung's exploration of the deeper invisible strata of human consciousness was not without some limits. Even he refrained from venturing too far into the world of spirituality. He generally discounted claims, such as those made by the Eastern spiritual traditions and Western mystics like Teresa of Avila and many others, that it is possible to transcend our mind and become conscious in the deepest core of the unconscious, beyond even the deep conditioning of time and space, birth and death.

So our journey through the unknown interior realms of our being will take us deeper and further than Jung was prepared to go. Nonetheless, we acknowledge his vital contribution and build on the foundations that he laid.

EGO AND NON-EGO

The word 'ego' in depth psychology is often used to refer to the conscious mind, which is naturally identified as 'I' or the personal self. Ego exists in relation to the larger psyche, the universal foundations of consciousness that underlie and support our individual awareness. Jung sometimes called this psychic substratum, which is submerged in deep unconsciousness, the 'non-ego'. The non-ego, according to this usage, is that depth of our being which is not conscious, and which can never be 'known' by our human mind or intellect. It is the mystery that lays behind the surface of our life and our being.

I like to think of my ego or mind as a small island that rises above the surface of the ocean. I am just one of millions of these little islands. Because this ocean is turbid and constantly moving to and fro I cannot see below the surface of the water. I only concern myself with what is above the water's surface. But if I could peer deep into the water,

I would see that I am really part of a great ridge of earth that seems to have no end, and out of which all the little islands poke up. The surface of the water is like the threshold of our consciousness. We cannot see what is in the unconscious. Our minds are too agitated, moving to and fro all the time. We only see what is above the water.

That great ridge of land under the water is the true support for my existence and that of all the other little islands. It is the 'non-ego'. It is not 'I', my personal self, because its nature is universal, not personal. But it is the substance and source of my being. If the water were to become perfectly clear and still, I would see that I really 'am' this endless ridge of land rather than just a tiny island amidst millions of other little islands dotting the great sea. It is not a perfect analogy, but at least it conveys something of the nature of ego and non-ego, conscious and unconscious.

'PROJECTING' THE UNCONSCIOUS INTO THE WORLD OF IMAGES AND EXPERIENCES

Jung was interested in what he called 'projection', the process by which the energies and contents of the unconscious are given visible conscious form in the images, stories, and experiences of our imagination, and even of our waking life. He focused his attention on dreams and myths as projections of the unconscious, but also was aware that all our experiences in life are, in a sense, symbolic in nature. They point to a deeper psychic meaning and significance, because they arise as projections and concretizations of the interplay of unconscious forces that shape our whole being within and without.

Much of our work in traveling through the interior realms of our being will be directed toward overcoming the automatic, unconscious nature of the process of projection. Meditation and spiritual practice in general are specifically focused on withdrawing the projection of psychic energy from the normal channels of thinking, perceiving, imagining, and so on, that we call our mind-process. To the degree that we are successful in this task, our mind becomes increasingly clear, calm, and transparent. Gradually, psychic energy builds in the unconscious until it has the power to break through the wall separating our consciousness from the deep unconscious. That is the process of 'awakening' or spiritual 're-birth'.

We will be exploring this dynamic interplay of ego and non-ego in greater depth as we discuss the seven chakras and seven dwelling places of the 'interior castle'. These two spiritual systems lend themselves to an interpretation that is consistent with the conscious/unconscious, ego/non-ego polarity that lay at the heart of depth psychology. Our careful 'weaving' together of psychology and spirituality will throw some new light on our subject, which is the development of the full potential of our individual consciousness. May each of us find here, a little fresh inspiration and insight for our own journey.

**MAPS CAN BE USEFUL
TO EXPLORERS**

The journey of spiritual development is truly an exploration of the unknown. To reach true peace, 'unending' peace, seems, at times, nearly impossible. Somehow, though, it is within our grasp. The very depth of the challenge forces us to grow beyond all that we have imagined that we are or can be. I am walking on my path, as you are on yours. Each of us must find our own way, and each person's path is unique.

☙

Yet there are universal principles of psychological and spiritual development that govern the nature of every path. In exploring kundalini yoga and *Interior Castle* through the lens of depth psychology, we are accessing a great storehouse of spiritual wisdom. My task and yours, if you desire it, is to discover how this deep and powerful vision is relevant to our own journey, to our own experiences as we face the inevitable challenges of our path.

No map, of course, however detailed or precise, can replace the knowledge gained through real first-hand exploration of the interior dimensions of consciousness. Each of us who desires the deepest fulfillment must discover anew the path of inner unfolding and realization. Maps can help us chart our course and provide some indication that we are traveling in a direction that will take us toward our desired destination.

Chapter 2

The Symbolism of Kundalini Yoga

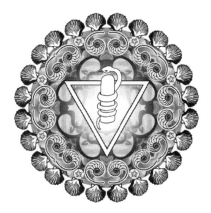

"Human reality is a consciousness-continuum evolving through a hierarchy of more and more comprehensive awareness of reality."

HARIDAS CHAUDHURI, IN *Philosophy of Meditation*

CONSCIOUSNESS POTENTIALS[1]

The spiritual development of individual consciousness through deeper and more universal states of awareness and psychic integration underlies the whole vision of the chakras that is central to kundalini yoga. This system, beginning at the base chakra and extending upward along the spinal column to the crown chakra, is a map of the human psyche, from its surface in the whirring images, sensations, thoughts, and feelings that we call our conscious mind to the deepest hidden core of our being, buried under layer upon layer of unconsciousness. It is also a map of consciousness development, laying out in successive order, the stages that a spiritual aspirant passes through on the journey to true peace.

Chakras represent potentials that are inherent in our being, but that are normally inactive or unrealized. They only become active as kundalini is aroused and awakened from its sleeping state and travels upward, opening and energizing each chakra as it passes through, coming to rest finally in the crown chakra, the 'thousand-petaled' lotus as it is called. When our life-energy is deliberately and consistently directed toward spiritual development, gradually kundalini or the dormant spiritual force within our psyche is activated, and we actualize all our hidden potentials for greatly expanded and deepened consciousness.

The journey of kundalini from the base to the crown chakra is an ascent, from states or realms of consciousness that are heavily conditioned and limited in scope to others that are more and more conscious, open, unconditioned, and universal.[2] The basic system of kundalini yoga, as encoded in the chakra system, is a universally valid model for the spiritual development of consciousness. The territory that it maps out must be explored and traversed by all of us whose spiritual desire is awakened and who apply ourselves with faith and devotion to a path of development, regardless what tradition or culture we are associated with. A study of kundalini yoga can help reveal the universal processes of transformation by which our human consciousness is gradually integrated at progressively deeper and more fundamental levels.

In the abstract symbolism of the chakras, the ascent of kundalini up the axis of the chakras conveys only that this is a developmental process, that our normal body-and-mind-based consciousness is the starting point for our spiritual transformation and development. That the second chakra is 'higher' than the first implies that if we become conscious at this depth of our being we have developed, psychologically and spiritually, beyond the realm of the first chakra. This development occurs by gaining control over the unconscious forces that cause us to think, feel, perceive, and act in the ways that we do. As we master those forces closest to the surface of our awareness, then we can gradually work to gain control over deeper and more powerful forces, one 'level' at a time, on up through the whole chakra system.

THE 'TRANS-DIMENSIONALITY' OF CHAKRAS

Chakras seem to mysteriously connect all levels of human reality, being at once physiological, psychical, and spiritual or transcendental in their totality. Their symbolic trans-dimensional nature defies intellectual analysis and discourages the tendency to interpret them in simplistic terms. For example, to view chakras only as 'energy' centers within the human body, as some popular treatments of kundalini yoga have been inclined to do, is to divest them of their supra-rational symbolic nature. Physiology by itself knows nothing about chakras because they are not material entities.[3] We will never find them by dissecting the human body, no matter how refined our instruments are.

The chakra system is grounded in an understanding of reality that is not divided into the separate categories of physiological, psychological, and spiritual. It does not entertain any notion of separate levels of reality. The view of chakras within the human body is, not only a picture of the human psyche as well, but also a picture of the whole universe, the cosmos in its entirety. All these are one indivisible reality, which appears, when viewed through our conditioned human mind, as the separate realms of body, psyche, and universe. The idea that the universe *in potentia* is contained or reflected in the human body is an ancient esoteric doctrine in both the East and West. The chakra system is a map of reality that sees the whole and represents it as a series of stages in the unfolding of consciousness.[4]

CHAKRAS, PERSONALITY DEVELOPMENT, AND THERAPY

Chakras are also being interpreted in the West as a model of holistic personality development.[5] Each chakra is equated with a primary stage of healthy self development: survival, sexuality, power, love, communication, intuition, and wisdom. Because chakras are trans-dimensional in nature, they have relevance and validity on many levels. So I see no harm in using them in this way. But this understanding of chakras is limited in depth and does not reflect their true significance as a system of the most complete and profound spiritual development.

Certain physical, emotional, and energetic symptoms are now viewed, in some therapeutic circles, as a kind of kundalini awakening, and thereby treated positively as indications of inner transformation rather than as dysfunctional or pathological states. This makes sense, provided that those who have such experiences and those professionals who support them understand that these are symptomatic stirrings of kundalini that can occur for any number of reasons and are not even remotely close to a full awakening of the spiritual potential that is latent within us. People who, for example, have a blissful vision or experience of opening the heart chakra, may not developmentally have progressed beyond the base chakra. Catching a glimpse of a higher level is not at all the same as being developmentally established at that level.

THE YOGA THEORY OF THE SUBTLE BODY

In yoga theory, chakras are energy centers of the 'subtle body', a kind of psycho-energetic field that connects the physical body with the transcendental spiritual reality that underlies all existence. The subtle body regulates the activities of *prana*, which expresses itself as the various energy systems of our body and as all forms of psychic energy. *Prana* is a Sanskrit term that refers to the source and essence of all energy in the universe. In relation to human beings, it signifies the life-force or vital energy which animates our body and mind, and all the systems thereof.

The idea of the subtle body is related to the Western concept of the unconscious. It is our unconscious mind that controls all the vital functions of our body. Psychic energy resides in the unconscious as well. Some yogis are known to gain an amazing degree of conscious control over such unconscious functions as the heartbeat and breathing. This is proof that *prana* or the vital energy of the body can be controlled through concentration.

AWAKENING THE SLEEPING KUNDALINI SERPENT

A chakra, then, is a constellation or integration of *prana* reflecting a particular state or level of consciousness within the developmental spectrum represented by the whole system. In the base chakra where spiritual development begins, kundalini is asleep. Even though we are conscious beings in possession of many cognitive capacities, we are 'spiritually unconscious' as we live our normal personal life in the world. We have no realization yet of our true nature: infinite, eternal, always established in peace. This is where we all begin our journey.

Symbolically represented as a serpent coiled at the base of the spine in the base or 'root' chakra, kundalini sleeps until aroused through sustained and intense spiritual practice. Once aroused, the kundalini serpent begins to uncoil and move upward into a secret channel, *sushumna* in Sanskrit, in the very center of the spine where the chakras are located. While asleep in the root chakra, the mouth of the coiled kundalini serpent closes off the entrance to this subtle channel through which the awakened or spiritualized *prana* flows upward to higher centers. When aroused, it advances up through the chakras, which signify stages in the deepening illumination and unification of our whole psyche, conscious and unconscious. As kundalini ascends up this axis to the crown chakra, we gradually open ourselves to the realization of our heavenly, immortal, and pure nature.

The concentration and activation of the core energy of our being that occurs through dedication to spiritual development awakens the deeper potentials within the unconscious. These are normally 'closed off' or inaccessible. As these potentials become actualized, we grow more conscious and gain a greater degree of self-mastery, having 'taken back' some of the power and influence of unconscious forces within us. Eventually, after much growth and transformation, we can become conscious 'as' spirit, and the 'peace that passeth all understanding' becomes our permanent blessing.

JUNG'S INSIGHT INTO THE SYMBOLIC NATURE OF THE CHAKRAS

Kundalini yoga is presented through the medium of symbols. The mandala-based imagery of the chakras, the slumber of the kundalini serpent, its awakening and ascent to the crown chakra, all tap into the deep archetypal structure of the psyche. As symbols, they integrate body, mind, and spirit into a unified and indivisible whole. In his kundalini yoga seminars in 1932, Carl Jung gave one of the best descriptions of the symbolic nature of the chakras that I have ever encountered:

> A symbol, then, is a living *Gestalt*, or form—the sum total of a highly complex set of facts which our intellect cannot master conceptually, and which therefore cannot be expressed in any way other than by the use of an image. . . . So, too, the cakras are symbols. They symbolize highly complex psychic facts which at the present moment we could not possibly express except in images. The cakras are therefore of great value to us because they represent a real effort to give a symbolic theory of the psyche.
>
> . . .The symbols of the cakra, then afford us a standpoint that extends beyond the conscious. They are intuitions about the psyche as a whole, about its various conditions and possibilities. They symbolize the psyche from a cosmic standpoint. It is as if a superconsciousness, an all-embracing divine consciousness, surveyed the psyche from above.[6]

Jung's insight into the significance of the chakras was profound. As he suggests, chakra symbolism presents a vision of human consciousness from a perspective far beyond our intellect's capacity to see trans-dimensional 'wholes'. That such a powerful symbolic system even exists can only indicate its evolution and elaboration by sages who tapped a depth and height of consciousness within which the whole psyche could be intuitively 'seen'.

More than any other person in the history of the modern West, Jung is responsible for opening our collective eyes to the reality of the unconscious, the vast unknown substructure of consciousness out of which our individual self-awareness arises. He was able to see that chakras present a map or topography of the psyche, and that symbolically they represent the transformation of consciousness and its re-integration at deeper and more universal levels of psychic interiority. Jung worked throughout his life to grasp the power of symbols in human consciousness. Depth psychology, with its focus on the relationship between conscious and unconscious, uses a language that can illumine the significance of the complex and profound symbolic system of kundalini yoga.

THE POLAR NATURE OF THE CHAKRA SYSTEM

Chakra symbolism presents a polar view of the human psyche. *Muladhara*, the 'root' chakra, located anatomically at the base of the spine, is at one end of the 'consciousness continuum', while *sahasrara*, the crown chakra, pictured at or slightly above the very top of the head, represents the other pole. It is a picture of the conscious-unconscious polarity of the human psyche. The lowest chakra is our normal state of consciousness in which we live our personal life in the world. The crown chakra is the core of our being, the deepest center of the unconscious, hidden from our awareness by many layers of unconscious conditioning.

Jung explained to his audience in the 1932 seminars that the 'map' of the chakras appears upside down to the

Western mind. Here the concreteness of material reality, and the powers of our analytic mind to manipulate it, have been accorded the highest value and are considered the apex in the long evolutionary development of human consciousness from its primal origins. In the system of kundalini yoga, this supposedly 'advanced' state of individual consciousness, which we all take completely for granted, is placed in the lowest position of development. In the base chakra, the spiritual potentials of our consciousness are 'asleep' or not yet activated.

If the higher chakras represent deeper levels of the personal and universal unconscious, then they present the possibility of unifying the two poles of our being, although the transformation required to do so is far from easy. The implication is, as Jung so clearly saw, that we develop ourselves psychologically and spiritually by 'entering into' and integrating our consciousness at deeper and deeper levels of the unconscious. Of course, he was attracted to this symbolic system that validated the basic vision underlying his own understanding of self-development.

A SNAPSHOT OF THE JOURNEY UP THROUGH THE CHAKRAS

Rather than going 'down' into the unconscious as we customarily speak and think in the West, in the system of kundalini yoga we travel 'up' into the unconscious. The root chakra, at the lower pole of the chakra axis, represents our consciousness in its fully conditioned, personalized, externalized state. It is the separate, person-identified, embodied consciousness that we all experience as normal and take completely for granted. In this realm of everyday reality, the personal self as subject experiences the world as object. We are identified with our body and our mind, with our sensations, feelings, thoughts, imaginings, perceptions, and so on. At each higher chakra increasingly deeper, more subtle and universal levels of unconscious conditioning are encountered.

In the root chakra, kundalini or the invisible spiritual power hidden within our being remains asleep. The power to transcend the narrow boundaries of our personal identity is dormant, buried deep within the unconscious like an unsprouted seed buried deep within the earth. Through a serious commitment to spiritual practice and the cultivation of inner life, this spiritual power is aroused. In the second chakra, we enter the 'watery' realm of instinct and unconscious tendencies, and slowly gain a degree of conscious mastery over these powerful interior forces. Working in the third chakra involves the capacity to recollect and focus our whole conscious being into a 'fire' of single-minded purpose, igniting a spiritual passion and resolve that has tremendous momentum.

The heart chakra or fourth realm of spiritual development marks the beginning of the 'awakening' process, a kind of momentary stepping outside of our own mind and our own 'self' into the vast, infinite realm of the deep unconscious. In the fifth chakra a state of deep interior absorption is reached in which our attention is completely withdrawn from our body and senses and deeply focused within. With our mind-process slowed way down and almost fully under our conscious control, now we begin to wake up or become conscious, deep in the unconscious, far beyond the everyday realm of personal identity. These spiritual experiences are tremendously powerful, and when repeated often, they transform us in the most fundamental way.

The sixth chakra represents a realm of universal consciousness, a state in which our awareness becomes so pure and undistracted that it now 'sees' its own divine and universal nature. And finally, upon reaching the crown chakra, complete unity is realized. The ancient split between conscious and unconscious, and between subject and object, disappears as does darkness with the rising sun. We know ourselves as pure and unconditioned, the infinite spiritual reality that was always our deepest truth, the very heart of life and of all creation.

The chakra axis marks formative levels in the universe of consciousness, both in the microcosm of the human psyche and in the vast macrocosm. Along this axis we travel from the personal to the universal, from conditioned to unconditioned, from finite to infinite, from bound to liberated, from partial consciousness to complete consciousness, from fear to true peace.

EACH CHAKRA, A 'REALM' OF CONSCIOUSNESS DEVELOPMENT

Each one of the lower five chakras is associated with one of the five fundamental 'elements' that in Indian metaphysics comprise the basic structural levels of reality. Beginning with earth at the root chakra, they move upward to water, fire, air, and ether at the progressively higher chakras. Earth is considered the most solid and material of the five basic elements that comprise manifest reality. In this cosmology, earth is derived from water, water from fire, fire from air, and air from ether or space, the most subtle and pervasive of all the elements. These are not elements in the Western sense of that word. The Sanskrit word is *tattva*, a primary category or state of reality. Each *tattva*, and therefore each corresponding chakra, is a 'world', a fundamental realm of existence.

The earth realm of the base chakra contains enfolded within it all the other realms because it is the most manifest realm. It is the concrete universe of matter, or rather the body-mind-self based consciousness that perceives the physical world. The next higher chakra is the water realm. When we are in the earth realm, we do not see the water realm. It is the next level of interiority in the structure of the cosmos and the human psyche. In other words it represents a deeper strata of reality than the solid earth realm that we experience through our senses. The earth realm evolves out of the water realm, in a causal sense. And so on, to the fire realm, the air realm, and the ether realm. The sixth and seventh chakras lay deeper, again in the causal sense, than all of these realms.

And so the basic nature of the universe is encoded in this system. Of course, because cosmos and psyche are one seamless reality in kundalini yoga, this is as much as anything a statement about the nature of consciousness. The manifest universe is consciousness externalized, while the inner world of the human psyche is consciousness internalized. Chakras, then, present a symbolic vision of the whole psyche, and a map for the development of consciousness, and the unification of the ego/non-ego poles of the psyche. To open a chakra on the upward journey of kundalini is to become conscious at that level of depth with the structure of the psyche, and the universe. Each chakra is an actual stage of spiritual realization.

In the teachings of kundalini yoga, the ego or finite personal consciousness, symbolized by the root chakra, contains within its deep hidden center an unknown spiritual power. Through devotion to spiritual development this power can be aroused and activated. Eventually we can awaken, or become conscious, in the deep universal core of our being through a process of purifying, transforming, and eventually transcending our personal, body-and-mind-based consciousness. Symbolized as the awakening of the kundalini serpent, its upward ascent, piercing one-by-one the chakras and opening their lotus buds, this is a developmental 'growth' in our capacity to be conscious at levels previously unimagined.

THE 'COILED-UP' ENERGY

The Sanskrit word *kundalini* literally means 'coiled up'. The serpent is coiled three and one-half times as she sleeps deep in the hidden center of the root chakra. Snakes, in general, have long been recognized as universal symbols of psychic energy. Kundalini can be thought of as the coiled or potential energy of consciousness development that is inherent but latent in all beings. The coiled, sleeping state of kundalini symbolizes the fact that the core energy of our being, our life-force, is buried in the unconscious. Yes, we breathe, we eat, we think and feel, but we are unconscious of our true nature. We are only conscious in a very limited way.

Deep in the core of our being, far below the surface of our awareness, a tremendous reservoir of psychic energy resides. This energy is in a potential state, as the energy in a coiled up spring is also potential energy that is only released in the process of uncoiling. With the core energy of our psyche in this potential state, we live through our identification with our body and mind. That is our deep, universal human conditioning. That is the 'coiled up' state of our psychic life. If that core life energy becomes 'uncoiled' or fully 'deconditioned', we become 'completely conscious', conscious as infinite Life.

☙

From our human perspective, it is easy to see how the consciousness of less evolved forms of life is bounded by the limitations of those forms. Ant consciousness, for example, can only exist within certain definite limits. It can't be cow consciousness. Just as cow consciousness can only be what it is, and not human consciousness.

Although we may not normally be aware of this, our human consciousness, albeit more evolved in cognitive ability than ant or cow consciousness, is still completely circumscribed by its human conditioning. We cannot be something other than a mortal human being. Our lives are lived according to the predetermined laws of nature. We are born from our mother's womb, we grow, have various life experiences, and then die. We cannot escape that natural cycle. In the coiled, latent state kundalini, the hidden core energy of our being, manifests as the cycle of birth and death and all that it entails.

Our personal life is completely lived within the boundaries of the conditioned human mind and body. "I am this body. I am a man or woman. I am these thoughts, feelings, sensations, perceptions, and so on, that I call my mind. I am a separate person with my own history, desires, fears, etc." We may not actually think these thoughts, but they are implicit in our consciousness. They represent the fundamental conditioning of the human psyche. It is a closed system. The energy of consciousness is coiled up, held tight within the clutches of natural law. Nature has brought us to the human level of evolution, where we are imprisoned for we cannot be other than an embodied, finite being with a human form and human capacities.

Of course, we seldom think of ourselves in this way. We prefer to think that we represent the pinnacle of nature's evolutionary plan. Spiritual traditions, however, are quick

ೞ

to point out that we are far from free, that fear is ever-present in us, and that death poses an inescapable question to us regarding our very identity, our life purpose, and our finiteness. Depth psychology, too, reminds us how 'unconscious' we really are, how our consciousness is completely molded and shaped by unconscious forces, that because they are hidden from our sight, are all the more powerful. Were we all fully conscious there would be no fear, anger, or violence present in this world of ours.

THE UNCOILING OF PSYCHIC ENERGY

From ancient times, human beings have found this situation disturbing and have sought a deeper and more lasting significance to their life and being. So religions are born, and quests of all kinds. But it is not until each one of us alone, within the depths of our own being, discover a growing desire to be free, to abide in fearlessness and peace and compassion for all life, that we begin a journey that will uncoil this deep impersonal energy of life and consciousness within us and release its true power.

The yoga tradition, and I believe, all spiritual traditions, point us toward the possibility of continuing the process of evolution that nature has begun. Our consciousness has unfolded to the human level, but that is far from the end of our journey. It is possible for each of us to not only continue that evolution, but to complete it. The question is 'how?'

Kundalini yoga answers that question, in its own way. It says that kundalini, the evolutionary energy of consciousness, although asleep in our normal body/mind identity, can be aroused and uncoiled, and its potency released as we develop the capacity to gain mastery over our conditioning, eventually reaching *sahasrara*, the thousand-petaled lotus, where we become fully conscious as pure, unconditioned, uncreated spiritual Being. Each chakra represents a level of conditioning that must be mastered and transcended in our evolutionary ascent. Psychologically, the 'coils' of unconscious conditioning must be forced open, for it is these various levels of conditioning that hide the spiritual Reality that is our true nature and create the experience we all share of finite, embodied personal existence.

The coiled state of the kundalini serpent depicts the tightly bound and heavily conditioned state of the fundamental energy of the human psyche. Until kundalini is aroused through spiritual desire and practice, no development of consciousness can take place. Whole 'realms' of unconscious conditioning are laid bare and transcended with the piercing of each chakra and the opening of its folded lotus blossoms. Sir John Woodruffe, author of *The Serpent Power*, a classic but very difficult to understand commentary on kundalini yoga, states: "Yoga thus works towards a positive state of pure consciousness by the negation of the operation of the principle of unconsciousness which stands in the way of its uprising."

UNTYING THE KNOTS OF THE PSYCHE'S CONDITIONING

Progressing through the chakras can be thought of as untying the 'knots' of conditioning by which the energy of the human psyche is bound, beginning with the most surface level of personal conditioning and moving, one knot at a time, to deeper and more universal levels of conditioning. Lama Govinda recounts a wonderful story of the Buddha teaching the path of liberation by tying a silk handkerchief in a series of six knots and then inquiring of Ananda, his close disciple, how the knots could be untied.[7] In the end Ananda sees that they can only be untied in the reverse order to which they were originally tied. This is a process of undoing whole realms of conditioning by which our core life energy, pure and unlimited in its own nature, becomes veiled by unconsciousness and projected into the 'hurly-burly' of our mind-process and our identity as an embodied personal self in a world of billions of other selves, all running around looking for 'something'.

The opening of the chakras, then, represents a re-integration of our being at progressively deeper levels of the personal and universal unconscious. To unify our psyche completely is to become fully and permanently conscious in the eternal spiritual core of our being while still retaining the capacity to function effectively at all other psychic levels.

As my own spiritual teacher, Baba Hari Dass, told me once in a private interview: "We are only partially conscious. When kundalini awakens we become fully conscious." The journey of kundalini to the crown chakra completes the cycle of creation. It is our destiny. And it is an adventure that awaits any and all of us who yearn for some greater fulfillment and peace than seems available in the fleeting images of this world that flash across the screen of our minds as we travel on the highway of life-experience.

ଓଃ

Chapter 3

Many Dwelling Places in the Castle of the Psyche

"Today while beseeching our Lord to speak for me because I wasn't able to think of anything to say nor did I know how to begin to carry out this obedience, there came to my mind what I shall now speak about, that which will provide us with a basis to begin with. It is that we consider our soul to be like a castle made entirely out of a diamond or of very clear crystal, in which there are many rooms, just as in heaven there are many dwelling places."

TERESA OF AVILA,
AT THE BEGINNING OF *Interior Castle*[1]

A JOURNEY TO THE SECRET CENTER OF OUR BEING

*B*ased on this simple but powerful analogy, the sixteenth-century Carmelite nun Teresa of Avila wrote her most famous work, *Interior Castle*. Proceeding from the dim outer courtyard of the castle, she describes the spiritual aspirant's journey of transformation through seven 'dwelling places' of the soul, each more interior than the previous one. The completion of this spiritual journey is the union of individual consciousness with God, who resides in the deepest secret center, the most interior dwelling place of our being. In Teresa's image-rich language, the journey's end is to become one with 'His Majesty', the 'King', the 'Sun Himself' whose light illumines the whole castle. We can only enter within the castle, in other words, can only penetrate the hidden depth of our own being, Teresa says, through prayer and meditation.

Written in language that is unique to the religious culture in which Teresa lived, and often expressed in a wealth of images and analogies, *Interior Castle* is a mine of spiritual psychology. She describes each of the dwelling places according to the nature of the inner life and spiritual awareness that unfolds at that stage, providing rich insight into the journey of consciousness development. Teresa uses the word 'soul' to refer to the unknown interior depth of our being and consciousness, whereas I primarily use the word 'psyche', to be consistent with the language of depth psychology. The meaning is the same.

Teresa describes the path leading into the hidden realms of the soul or psyche as neither a descent nor an ascent, but as a journey inward, from the outer surface of consciousness to its innermost core. The image itself, of entering into the castle, exploring the various rooms that comprise each level, then progressing further into the heart of the great castle, finally reaching the seventh level, the very center, where the Lord of the Castle resides, beautifully portrays the vast interiority of consciousness that normally remains hidden to our sight, or unconscious.

THE PSYCHE AS CRYSTALLINE CASTLE

It is a symbolism that depth psychology finds natural and irresistible, the psyche as a crystalline castle with almost endless, hidden inner chambers, a radiant light emanating from its deepest secret center. I am immediately reminded of the description of the 'New Jerusalem' in the Book of Revelations in the New Testament. Here the liberated soul is pictured as a walled city that "glittered like some precious jewel of crystal clear diamond. The city did not need the sun or the moon for light, since it was lit by the radiant glory of God."

The crystalline castle is a powerful symbol of psychic wholeness and unity. Jung might have said that it represents the 'archetype' of wholeness that is found in a variety of forms in the myths, symbols, and images of all cultures. This image clearly arises out of a deep collective strata in the human psyche. The symbol of the crystalline castle with its inner source of illumination reflects the structure of the psyche and the potential for its unification. Teresa outlines for us how we may travel from the surface of our mind, the outer courtyard, to our deeply hidden self-luminous core, the seventh and most interior dwelling place, where the true 'Dweller' within us resides in complete secrecy. When we complete this journey, we are whole, we are one with the Mystery of all existence.

☙

DWELLING IN 'MY FATHER'S HOUSE'

Within this wholeness, this unity of consciousness, there are many rooms. In the famous line quoted at the beginning of this chapter in which Teresa lays out her essential vision, the reference to the many dwelling places of heaven is undoubtedly taken from the verse in the New Testament Gospel According to John 14:2: "In my Father's house there are many places to live in." The word 'mansions' is often used here, rather than 'places to live in' or 'dwelling places', but that is a loose figurative translation of the original Greek. In any event, we can understand these dwelling places as signifying states in which our individual consciousness can dwell or live.

In the passage containing this verse, Jesus is reassuring his disciples that although he will be taken away from them, he is going to prepare a place for them, in his 'Father's house', so they may be with him. Jesus is speaking here as the spiritually realized consciousness, as the divine core of his own being and all existence. In Teresa's language, he is speaking as 'His Majesty', the 'Lord of the castle', the 'Inner Sun', and so on, who dwells in our most secret interior depth.

Jesus is telling those souls who are greatly devoted to Him that if they 'know' him, they will 'know' the Father and dwell in his house, the 'kingdom of heaven'. To know 'Him' is to be fully conscious, to have completed the journey to the center of our being as he, the man Jesus, completed the journey to the center of his own being. All separateness, all unconsciousness, and all duality are then transcended. We are in the 'Father's house'. We are consciously and indissolubly one with the heart or core reality of all existence.

ॐ

When Jesus' disciples tell him that they do not know where he is going or the way there, he replies, "I am the Way; I am Truth and Life. No one can come to the Father except through me. If you know me, you will know my Father too." In other words, it is only through the realization of our own infinite, pure, eternal nature that we come into conscious union with the spiritual reality that lays behind the whole universe of name and form. In Jesus' words this reality, without beginning or end, is called the 'Father within'.

Using language and images that perhaps the people of his day, at the very least his own disciples, would grasp, Jesus in this dialogue lays out the essential requirement for spiritual realization: to 'know Me', to become fully conscious as the eternal spiritual essence of our being. Then we will 'know my Father' as well, we will be consciously one with the Truth underlying all creation. The whole of *Interior Castle* is based on this theme: to become consciously one with the true spiritual source deep within us, hidden from our sight by layer upon layer of unconscious conditioning.

THE GREAT AND SUBLIME BEAUTY OF THE CASTLE

It is of great significance, I believe, that Teresa compares the many 'abodes' of the soul or individual consciousness to the many dwelling places in heaven, or the Father's house. In the opening paragraph of *Interior Castle*, immediately following the famous line in which she compares the soul to a castle, she goes on to comment on the incomparable beauty of the spiritual depth within us:

☙

> For in reflecting upon it carefully, Sisters, we realize that the soul of the just person is nothing else but a paradise where the Lord says He finds His delight. So then, what do you think that abode will be like where a King so powerful, so wise, so pure, so full of all good things takes His delight? I don't find anything comparable to the magnificent beauty of a soul and its marvelous capacity. Indeed, our intellects, however keen, can hardly comprehend it, just as they cannot comprehend God; but He Himself says that He created us in His own image and likeness.

The castle of our psyche with its many rooms is deep and beautiful beyond all possibility of understanding, for it is as vast and unlimited as the spiritual reality underlying all creation. It is, in fact, the dwelling place of the Most High, although, of course, our limited conscious mind can in no way fully grasp this truth. Heaven, or the Father's house, becomes our dwelling place only through a complete conscious realization of the interior depth of our own being.

Teresa makes abundantly clear from the very beginning that only by entering into the various dwelling places, by becoming conscious at the various levels of psychic reality normally buried in unconsciousness, are we able to develop ourselves spiritually. Our human consciousness is made in the image of heaven, infinite in depth, yet having many invisible dwelling places, or states of being, within it. Upon finally reaching the seventh dwelling place "where the very secret exchanges between God and the soul take place" we become conscious in the deepest center of our being. We are one with God, or 'uncreated Spirit' as Teresa sometimes says. The evolutionary journey of consciousness is completed. We are conscious as the Whole of existence, the source and substance and reality of all that is.

> ෴

LEVELS OF INTERIORITY WITHIN THE 'CASTLE' OF THE PSYCHE

The seven levels of interiority in the castle represent stages in the progressive development of consciousness. Each stage is characterized by both an inner deepening and expansion of consciousness, and signals a new level of depth and wholeness in the integration of the psyche. In the very difficult journey into and through these 'mansions' or realms until the center, essence, and source of the psyche is reached, we, as dedicated spiritual aspirants, gradually penetrate the unconscious, activating its evolutionary energy and potential. At each level a re-integration, or powerful new synthesis, must take place so that our awareness is gradually transformed, becoming progressively more expansive, universal, and homogeneous, and less limited, localized, dispersed, and unconscious.

The first three realms are a preparation for entry into the more interior realms, into states of consciousness that transcend the normal capacities of our mind. These begin in the fourth realm. In order to create the conditions in which our awareness becomes sufficiently powerful to trigger a radical expansion of consciousness into our deep, unconscious, universal core, we must realize a rare degree of internal integration. To use a favorite word of Teresa, we must 'recollect' our psychic energy from its normal dispersion in many endless streams of thoughts, feelings, motivations, activities, and so on, then gradually mold it into an undistracted singleness of purpose. A steady and intense beam of unified purpose is required to free consciousness from our mind's relentless pull toward distracted involvement with the external activities and demands of life in the world.

మ

The fourth through seventh dwelling places in this long interior journey through the human psyche represent the processes of awakening by which our personal consciousness is lifted up, out of itself, into a depth that is utterly impersonal and universal, beyond all the 'knowing' processes of our mind. Gradually we penetrate deep into our own inner reality. Through our journey of transformation, we slowly learn to forsake all claim to a separate and substantive personal identity in order to be 'reborn' or 'awakened' at the spiritual level.

Upon reaching and becoming established in the innermost chamber of our being, our consciousness remains, on the inner level, always in total union with the deep Mystery that is its source and essence. On the outer level we work and play, promoting each in our own way, some visibly, others invisibly, the upliftment of humanity and the spiritual development of all beings.

TERESA'S RELIGIOUS LANGUAGE AND IMAGES

In interpreting the religious language of *Interior Castle* into the language of depth psychology, I follow Jung's lead. When we speak of God or spirit or the divine, we are referring psychologically to the reality of the deep unconscious. The very finiteness of our human mind gives rise to the awareness of its own limitation, and in all cultures that which lay beyond the boundaries of our knowledge and understanding has always been represented in mythic or archetypal images and symbols, and to some extent, in religious ideas.

For example, Teresa often addresses or calls that infinite source of life and consciousness that dwells in the deepest center of our being, 'His Majesty', whose splendor, wisdom, power, and goodness are incomprehensible to our finite mind. This and other religious designations are, psychologically, symbolic representations of the non-ego, the deep unknown 'background' within and without us, out of which we emerge as self-aware beings. We are conscious, but we are not conscious of the source and true nature of our being, nor of the universe as a whole. That mystery, that deep 'unknowingness', naturally finds expression in our imagination as Divinity in its many forms.

Following Biblical tradition, Teresa also personifies the power of unconsciousness within us as the devil, the prince of darkness. Many times she uses the plural, devils. In speaking of that person's consciousness who has 'fallen into mortal sin', she says that since the devil is 'darkness itself', this confused soul becomes covered by darkness as well. 'Mortal sin' here refers to intentions and actions that are rooted in a complete lack of awareness of the eternal source of being and of the sacred unity of all life. To grasp the power and universality of Teresa's teachings, it is necessary to translate her religious language into its psychological equivalent. Then we can feel more keenly just how 'alive' her words and images are.

Teresa often refers to the devil or devils as the forces within our mind that tempt, distract, or pull our attention away from a spiritual focus toward a 'worldly' focus. By worldly, she means lacking awareness of any spiritual purpose and motivated by personal desires and attachments. Such a state is one of spiritual 'darkness', she says, in which the power of unconsciousness holds sway over our mind.

HUMILITY AS THE FOUNDATION OF SPIRITUAL SEEKING

When we become devoted to spiritual development and attempt to enter into the interior dimensions of our being, soon enough we will encounter the psychological reality of this power, the devil, and will have to engage it in battle to become free from its tenacious grip. Otherwise we will find it very difficult to penetrate to any significant degree of interior depth. The 'enemy' appears in many different guises: as fear and anxiety, as all the 'grasping' tendencies of our mind, as fascination with our body and senses, as confusion and lack of clarity about life's purpose, as blame and judgment, as the blindness of believing that we are persons who have a real existence separate from the whole, as the lack of energy and initiative to undertake spiritual practice, and so on.

That is why Teresa insists over and over again on self-knowledge and humility as the necessary foundation for spiritual growth. Self-knowledge, for Teresa, means knowing that we are nothing in and of ourselves, that our life is actually the infinite, universal life hidden deep within our being. Our claim to a 'personal' life, she says, is made out of unconsciousness and delusion. One of the ways she teaches us to fight and overcome self-pride and all egocentric tendencies is to constantly remind ourselves that our human ego, our personal consciousness and identity, is nothing in itself.

Teresa's emphasis on humility can be easily misunderstood, especially given our modern Western distrust of language that tends to belittle our personal self. She often refers to herself in very apologetic terms, and suggests that human beings are nothing compared to the greatness and goodness of God. Her way was to become the 'slave' of God, who is the true Life of her life, the Self of her self, the very source and substance of her being. But God, or spirit, our true being, has nothing to do with the personal self, which is entirely a creation of our conditioned mind. While Teresa's style may not appeal to us now and may be somewhat altered to suit the needs of our time and conditioning, her insistence on humility is central to the development of consciousness that she describes.

ENTERING WITHIN THE INTERIOR CASTLE

In the following passage Teresa introduces the idea of entering within the castle, or entering into our own deep interiority:

> Well, getting back to our beautiful and delightful castle we must see how we can enter it. It seems I'm saying something foolish. For if this castle is the soul, clearly one doesn't have to enter it since it is within oneself. How foolish it would seem were we to tell someone to enter a room he is already in.

We are so accustomed to living on the surface of our being, with the energy of our consciousness focused on our body, mind, and world, that we can hardly imagine what 'entering within ourselves' might mean. How can we enter within our being, since we already are that being? The whole of *Interior Castle* is required to fully answer that question, but Teresa begins to answer it as she continues her dialogue:

> But you must understand that there is a great difference in the ways one may be inside the castle. For there are many souls who are in the outer courtyard—which is where the guards stay—and don't care at all about entering the castle, nor do they know what lies within that most precious place, nor who is within, nor even how many rooms it has.

Through the castle analogy, Teresa explains that our human consciousness is a multi-dimensional reality with various possibilities and degrees of self-awareness inherent in it. We are likely, she says, to spend our lives entirely living in the dim light of the outer courtyard of the castle. That is the realm in which our personal life in the world occupies our full attention, and we do not cultivate the spiritual potential that is hidden within us. Teresa laments this fate, in which we remain trapped in spiritual darkness, unaware of the deeper potentials of our being and uninterested in exploring them and seeking the profound fulfillment they offer. Then, she advises us how we can 'enter within ourselves':

> You have already heard in some books on prayer that the soul is advised to enter within itself; well, that's the very thing I'm advising . . . The door of entry into this castle is prayer and reflection.

PRAYER AND MEDITATION: THE PATH TO 'ENTER WITHIN OURSELVES'

Teresa uses the word 'prayer' to cover a whole range of meditative spiritual practices that gradually evolve as we work our way through the seven stages of development. Both the nature of the practice and the state of consciousness that accompanies it undergo a major transformation from the early to the latter stages. In the early going, prayer, Teresa says, is an active willful exercise in focusing our attention on a spiritual image or idea, or a scriptural truth, to the exclusion of all else. While it may at first begin as a spoken exercise, it becomes very quickly a silent, interior practice accompanied by much faith and devotion.

Proficiency in this practice leads us on to various states of concentration, called 'recollection', which in turn lead to deeper states of inner quiescence, finally culminating in complete 'union with God'. In these final stages of meditation, we are absorbed in the transcendent spiritual depths of our being and asleep to the world and to our normal body-mind-based consciousness. In the normal course of spiritual development, this progression or 'ripening' of spiritual practice, takes place through many years of devoted practice.

Interior prayer, as Teresa practiced and understood it, is a form of what we now call meditation, which can be defined as the disciplined practice of training our attention to remain steadily directed without interruption toward an inspired and interior focus. Over many years, we learn to continuously direct the beam of our attention toward a single inspired focus or purpose, which unifies all our energy of desire and will and devotion, until eventually all distracting thoughts and perceptions cease.

The word 'meditation' was used in a somewhat more restricted sense in Teresa's day and tradition. 'Discursive meditation' referred to a practice of active reflection, with the aid of concepts and thoughts, a kind of deep interior, highly focused contemplation on a spiritual idea. We can use our imagination and power of visualization in the same way. For example, a favored practice for Teresa during the early part of her development was imagining her soul or psyche as a garden in which Christ could walk and enjoy the blooming flowers that represented the spiritual qualities she was attempting to cultivate.

In contrast to its normal current usage, the word 'contemplation' was used in Teresa's time and tradition to refer to deep meditation in which our normal mind-process of thinking, perceiving, and so on, is nearly or completely suspended, and we consciously enter into the interior, non-personal depth of our being. This is what Teresa means by 'entering within ourselves'. She uses the word 'supernatural' to describe meditation and spiritual experiences that contain some degree of transcendence, implying that these states are supra-rational and non-egoic in nature and origin.

FROM DARKNESS TO LIGHT, FROM UNCONSCIOUSNESS TO COMPLETE CONSCIOUSNESS

Entering into the castle and penetrating its mysteries takes us on our journey in consciousness from a world of darkness, the outer courtyard, toward more and more light. The 'King' of the castle, who dwells in the seventh mansion, is called the 'Inner Sun', the source of all light, within and without the castle. Light radiates out from this deep hidden center, becoming progressively less intense, less bright, as the distance from its source increases. By the time it reaches the outermost rooms, it is very dim, and the outer courtyard is enveloped in semi-darkness; there, all is indistinct, shadowy, and foreign.

Psychologically, Teresa's image clearly places the source of all consciousness or light far within the depths of our psyche, in its hidden core. The process, then, of entering into the castle of our interior being is one of growing more and more conscious, becoming gradually less and less unconscious. At the end of our journey, we can become fully conscious, fully illumined, one with the eternal, unbounded essence of consciousness and life.

This increase of consciousness that accompanies entry into each interior realm must not be understood as an increase of knowledge in the discursive or intellectual sense. It is an increase of light, an opening into an expanded state of awareness, a greater capacity to see, not on the physical or mental plane, but spiritually. This increase represents a qualitative growth in our capacity to realize deeper, more hidden, and more universal causes and forces that form the basis of our life and consciousness. Gradually we acquire a greater depth of psychic integration and draw closer to the source of light and life within us.

Traveling through the interior mansions of our being necessitates the removal of the coverings or veils of unconscious conditioning that very effectively block the light of pure consciousness that emanates from the deepest center, or essence, of our being. These veils limit our normal experience to identification with the finite, separate, personal self-consciousness, with body, mind, and world.

'PEELING AWAY' THE LAYERS OF UNCONSCIOUS CONDITIONING

In describing the castle, Teresa says: "Think of how a palmetto has many leaves surrounding and covering the tasty part that can be eaten." I have never eaten a palmetto, but I believe that it is a kind of fruit in which the succulent edible core is covered over by many layers of leaves. Journeying through the many realms that underlie and give rise to our awareness requires us to become increasingly daring spiritual explorers. We dig deep to discover that which is hidden within us, and then fight to become conscious at depths of the unconscious that have been submerged in darkness for eons of human and pre-human evolution. At first, these layers of unconsciousness are more personal in nature, then when those are 'peeled away' or mastered, the more universal levels of conditioning that constitute the deep substratum of our awareness can be gradually entered, explored, and stripped away. This exploration is like a very deep archeological dig in the subliminal realms of our psyche.

ଔ

Undertaking such a daring journey of exploration will require more of us than we can imagine. It is the greatest challenge we can embrace. It is an exciting adventure that has the potential to fulfill completely all our deepest desires, hopes, and dreams. It will not be easy, but we will learn to relish the gradually deepening challenges it brings as we meet them, one by one, and enjoy the spiritual fruits that come with real growth and development of our true potential.

Teresa makes abundantly clear that the 'Inner Sun' dwells in all beings and radiates as the source of consciousness in the worst 'sinner' as well as the most saintly of beings. The difference between these two lay not in a greater presence of spirit in the saint, but in greater purity of heart and mind. In the consciousness of the spiritually realized being, all the conditions that block the light coming from the center of the psyche have been removed, 'peeled away'. In the consciousness of those of us who have yet to cultivate a deep spiritual awareness, though, the 'thick black cloth' of unconsciousness blocks out most of the light. Although we may be conscious of ourselves as persons and of the world, we remain completely unaware of the pure, luminous center and truth of our own being, and of the Unity of all life, all existence.

THE ANALOGY OF THE 'SPIRITUAL MARRIAGE'

At journey's end, when all the veils of unconsciousness have been penetrated and removed, the state of 'union' or complete consciousness is realized. We have then traveled all the way to the invisible, unknowable heart of the universe. Teresa refers to this state as one of 'spiritual marriage' in which our fully purified consciousness is indissolubly united with God, who is the 'spirit of the soul'.

The image of the spiritual marriage is one way of describing that state of wholeness and completeness toward which all life is unconsciously striving. Teresa characterized the stages preceding the actual marriage or union of our individual consciousness with God, our very source and substance, as those of courtship and betrothal, in which we meet and become acquainted with the 'Life of our life'. In the final marriage, our consciousness becomes one with its spiritual source, never again to be separate. We become conscious 'as' unborn, undying spirit, which is the true substance of the whole of creation.

DIFFERENT WAYS OF CHARACTERIZING THE SPIRITUAL IDEAL OF 'WHOLENESS'

Different traditions and teachers use various symbolic and metaphysical ways of pointing to and characterizing the ideal of wholeness, in the full spiritual sense of that word: *nirvana*, liberation, the kingdom of heaven, the promised land, the philosopher's stone, and so on. We may be inclined to argue that these represent quite different states or realities or goals. But no, that is not the case. Each, albeit in its own unique and wonderful way, points toward the same possibility for the development of our full consciousness potential.

Depth psychology also provides a way of understanding our potential for spiritual development. The polarity of conscious and unconscious, like the polarity of the 'outer courtyard' and 'innermost secret chamber' of the castle of our being, points us toward our deep potential for unity, wholeness, and complete consciousness.

Teresa's 'spiritual marriage' analogy gives us a familiar way to understand the final stages of spiritual development, which are very difficult to even talk about because they transcend our mind's capacity to 'know'. Her language is dualistic: two who were separate become one. Some traditions use language that is non-dualistic: we simply become conscious as that which we truly are, always have been, and always will be. In this way of describing spiritual realization, there never were two, self and Spirit, but only the illusion of two. Our separate personal self was only a 'phantom' created and sustained by the universal conditioning of our mind. Spirit alone is. There was only the illusion of duality and separateness.

These are differences of description, that is all. There are various ways of describing and characterizing spiritual realization. Teresa never fails to remind us that just as there are many rooms and dwelling places within the depths of our being, so there are many paths that lead to the Peace that cannot be understood by the finite human mind. True peace is the same, infinite in breadth and depth, no matter how we describe the path that leads us to it. We can learn to appreciate and learn from a variety of descriptions of 'wholeness' and the paths that lead to it.

SIMILARITY OF *INTERIOR CASTLE* AND KUNDALINI YOGA

However far apart in culture, style, temperament, and religious tradition *Interior Castle* is from the chakra system of kundalini yoga, their differences seem to pale into relative insignificance when both are viewed through the lens of depth psychology. Then the essential similarity of the vision upon which each of these well-known spiritual 'teachings' is based can be clearly seen. Both describe the depth dimension of consciousness in seven levels, from the surface of awareness to the innermost transcendent core. Both are models of the interior structure of consciousness, of the soul or psyche. And both are maps and guidebooks for the long journey of spiritual realization undertaken by those of us whose destiny leads us to seek the 'wholeness' and completion that our inner being demands.

They map the territory that we must traverse in order to gradually free ourselves from the many levels of conditioning that shape and mold every aspect of our experience of life. They lay out a path that takes us through the depth of our personal being, our desires and fears, and then far deeper into the universal foundations of our human consciousness. Finally, they inspire and encourage us to persevere until we are able to enter into and realize our identity as that unfathomable all-embracing mystery which is our very source, our life, our truth, our all-in-all.

The development of our individual consciousness, according to these two complementary visions, is at once a journey into the depths of our psyche, into its innermost center, and an ascent to the peak of spiritual wholeness. At journey's end, our mind or personal consciousness, is resolved into its infinite essence, just as a mountain stream finally reaches the ocean and empties into it, never again to be separate.

Chapter 4

Meditation and the Integration of the Psyche

"*Everyone must take time daily for quiet and meditation. In daily meditation lies the secret of power. No one can grow in either spiritual knowledge or power without it. Practice the presence of God just as you would practice music... It is the only way you will ever gain definite knowledge, true wisdom, newness of experience, steadiness of purpose, or power to meet the unknown... When we are consciously the Truth, it will radiate from us and accomplish the works without our ever running to and fro.*"

— EMILIE CADY, IN *Lessons in Truth*[1]

STOPPING THE MOVIE PROJECTOR OF OUR MIND

The purpose of meditation in spiritual development is to stop the movie projector of our mind. Much practice is necessary to reach the point where that becomes possible. In the ancient text called the Yoga Sutras, perhaps the most foundational scripture in the whole vast yoga tradition of India, yoga is defined in the famous line: *yoga cittavritti nirodha*. "Yoga is the cessation of the fluctuations of the mind." We have attained the state of yoga, or unity and wholeness, when our mind becomes steady and still. The Sanskrit word *nirodha* implies not only cessation, but also inhibition. In this sense, yoga is also the attempt made to slow down and finally stop the rapid fluctuations of our mind.

Our mind is the name we give to all our processes of sensing, perceiving, thinking, feeling, and so on, which collectively generate our moment-to-moment stream of consciousness. All of these processes are, in themselves, unconscious. They happen automatically. We have some limited choice as to what appears on the movie screen of our mind and how we respond to it, but even our choices are influenced by many powerful unconscious forces that we may have no cognizance of. And we cannot, try as we may, shut off our mind-process. That happens only in the state of deep dreamless sleep, when we are completely submerged in unconsciousness.

WHEN THE 'COVERING' OF OUR MIND IS REMOVED, WE SEE WHO WE REALLY ARE

In the yoga tradition, our mind is considered a kind of covering over the true nature of our being. Our mind, with its dualistic perception of self and world, is a manifestation of our universal human conditioning, generated by powerful unconscious forces deep within us. The purpose of meditation is to remove this covering. It does that by a continual attempt to withdraw the projection and dispersion of our core psychic energy into the processes of thinking, sensing, perceiving, and so on.

When the covering of the mind is completely removed, we become conscious as the infinite, divine Life that pervades all and is all. Then we are completely conscious. As long as we identify with our body/mind/personal self, we are only partially conscious. Our psychic energy is being projected into a tremendous diversity of body and mind-based processes. When, through a long course of inner discipline fueled by our spiritual desire, our psychic energy is totally withdrawn from these scattered channels, and intensely focused within, we eventually break through the barrier of our ego or mind-based consciousness and become conscious in the spiritual depths of our being, far beyond the realm of self and world.

We see then that not only is our personal self a mind-created illusion, but that the world we perceive is also a kind of waking dream, an appearance. Behind that appearance, hidden from our mind, is pure spirit, pure infinite Being. Our mind sees separateness, but behind that appearance of separateness is unbroken Unity.

The Bible expresses all this in the simple statement: "Be still, and know that I am God." When we attain conscious inner stillness, our true nature and that of the whole universe is revealed to us. We become conscious as the Whole, which we always were unconsciously. Nothing new is gained, only we remove our mind's covering of separateness, fear, and limitation. 'I' or 'I am' is the universal reflection of infinite, divine Consciousness in the mirroring waters of every human mind. In those murky, stirred up waters, we only see a partial reflection, the personal 'I' and its object, the world.

"TEACHING ATTENTION TO FLOW WITHOUT A BREAK" TOWARD A SINGLE FOCUS

So, meditation is a de-conditioning strategy, a method for 'recollecting' the energy of our consciousness that is normally divided and dispersed in many little streams of thought, worry, desire, imagination, and so on. Except for the state of deep, dreamless sleep our mind is truly a non-stop movie projector, generating a stream of consciousness that flies by with sometimes dizzying speed. Who is running that projector, I wonder? Some powerful unconscious forces, no doubt. Through meditation we can gradually gain control over those forces and operate the projector ourselves, as we choose to or not.

Eknath Easwaran, (1910-1999), a modern 'seer' and teacher of meditation, originally from southern India, who came to this country in 1959 and soon after started the Blue Mountain Center of Meditation in northern California, and who has written many excellent books on spiritual development, defines meditation as a "dynamic discipline" for "teaching attention to flow without a break toward a single inspirational focus in the mind."[2] The focus for meditation can be either an object, such as a sacred word, inspirational passage, or a visualization of some kind, or an activity, such as watching the breath, deep inner listening, keeping awareness of God's presence, 'witnessing' the mind's activity without getting involved in it, and so on.

Or it can be a combination of these, such as awareness of breath coordinated with concentration on internally repeated sounds and/or visualizations. There are various methods of meditation that use different kinds of interior focus, but the ultimate purpose of all of them is to bring our mind to a state of perfect steadiness, stillness and pure non-objectified awareness. "In this profound absorption the mind is still, calm, and clear. This is our native state. Once we become established in it, we know once and for all who we are and what life is for."[3]

SPIRITUAL PRACTICE: EXERTION TO ACHIEVE INNER STILLNESS AND TRANSPARENCY

In meditation practice, the unifying, integrating force is our intention to focus our mind's energy, using the method of our choice, and to discover the essential nature of our consciousness. That is the real object of concentration. The further we go in meditation, the more various techniques converge. Proficiency in any method depends upon how continuously and deeply we can hold to our purpose. Our unified will alone brings success in meditation. The whole thrust of spiritual practice is to unify our desires and will. This is accomplished by withdrawing the energy from many little desires and channeling it into one mega-desire: to awaken to spiritual reality, our true being, and the life of the universe.

Spiritual practice is defined in the Yoga Sutras as "exertion to acquire a tranquil state of mind devoid of fluctuations."[4] In the broadest sense, any disciplined activity that reduces our sense of personal separateness and consequently calms our mind can be considered spiritual practice. Worship, devotion to God, selfless service, mindfulness, limitation of desires, and other similar practices fall within the scope of this definition. All of these support the practice of meditation, which is the most direct and effective way to reach a state of awareness in which our mind is free of fluctuations.

It becomes gradually possible for those of us who practice meditation and other spiritual disciplines with total energy and dedication for many years, to master all the forces of the unconscious. Step by step, we unify our mind, integrating unconscious forces into our conscious control, preparing ourselves to 'wake up' in the universal, spiritual core of our being. It is as if we are gradually clarifying the murky, agitated waters of the lake of our mind. When this lake is completely clear, calm, and transparent, we are ready to 'see' into the infinite depths of our being.

VIGILANCE

Exiled Vietnamese Buddhist monk and well-known spiritual teacher, Thich Nhat Hahn, advises students of mindfulness meditation to:

> Be as awake as a person walking on high stilts—any mis-step could cause the walker to fall. Be like a medieval knight walking weaponless in a forest of swords. Be like a lion, going forward with slow, gentle, and firm steps. Only with this kind of vigilance can you realize total awakening.[5]

These powerful images capture better than any conceptual explanation the challenge of meditation practice. To cultivate the vigilance he describes, which is an undistracted focusing of our mind's energy, demands a unified will, a singleness of purpose, and a determination so thorough and so deep that all distracting thoughts, sensations, and perceptions gradually cease to interrupt the flow of our internalized attention.

If, for example, we are practicing an 'inner listening' meditation, we are attempting to become sufficiently quiet and inwardly receptive to 'hear' the spiritual presence within us, coming into our awareness from the unknown depths, far beyond the realm of our own mind. We move toward a concentrated or 'one-pointed' state as our 'inner listening' becomes continuous and free of distractions. It becomes painfully obvious to us that every distracting *vritti* or 'thought-wave' or fluctuation in our awareness constitutes a break in the continuous flow of our silent listening state.

DRAWING WATER BY HAND FROM A DEEP WELL

In discussing the nature of meditation and spiritual practice during the early phase of spiritual development, Teresa comments:

> Beginners in prayer, we can say, are those who draw water from the well. This involves a lot of work on their own part, as I have said. They must tire themselves in trying to recollect their senses. Since they are accustomed to being distracted, this recollection requires much effort. They need to get accustomed to caring nothing at all about seeing or hearing, to practicing the hours of prayer, and thus to solitude and withdrawal.

The comparison of this stage of meditation to drawing water, by hand, from a well refers to a famous analogy Teresa uses to illustrate how meditation changes as spiritual development progresses. She compares the aspiring soul to a garden in which many flowers and beautiful plants are beginning to grow:

> And with the help of God we must strive like good gardeners to get these plants to grow and take pains to water them so that they don't wither but come to bud and flower and give forth a most pleasant fragrance to provide refreshment for this Lord of ours. Then He will often come to take delight in this garden and find His joy among these virtues.

She outlines four ways of accomplishing this watering of the garden of the soul in which spiritual qualities are beginning to grow:

> It seems to me the garden can be watered in four ways. You may draw water from a well (which is for us a lot of work). Or you may get it by means of a water wheel and aqueducts in such a way that it is obtained by turning the crank of the water wheel. (I have drawn it this way sometimes—the method involves less work than the other, and you get more water.) Or it may flow from a river or a stream. (The garden is watered much better by this means because the ground is more fully soaked, and there is no need to water so frequently—and much less work for the gardener.) Or the water may be provided by a great deal of rain. (For the Lord waters the garden without any work on our part—and this way is incomparably better than all the others mentioned.)

WHEN OUR MIND-FIELD IS CALM, WE BEGIN TO 'FIND OUR OWN REST'

When we begin meditation and for some time thereafter, our mind process is so fast and furious that very little real interior concentration can occur. But we keep trying to wrangle our stream of consciousness into some manner of control and order. Gradually, through some years of devoted practice, our mind-process begins to slow down and we notice an increased ability to keep it steady for short periods. The space between our thoughts lengthens, and we are, at times, somewhat less 'involved' in our thoughts. As our mind slows down, we realize that it can engage in only one activity at a time, although by virtue of the speed and subtlety with which it functions, normally it appears to be doing several things at once.

Even the briefest fleeting thought or sense impression causes a disturbance or ripple in the energy field of our mind. When we are engaged in a thought or sense impression, however briefly, we cease to be focusing on our spiritual purpose. And conversely, when our inner focus is continuous, no other fluctuations are present in our mind-field. If we persevere for a long time, and gradually intensify our effort and, of course, our spiritual desire, we can become the master of our own mind. That is no small accomplishment.

Thich Nhat Hahn likens the 'one-pointed' state to that of a pebble thrown into a stream that, 'detached from everything', falls 'effortlessly' and comes to the point of complete rest on the fine sand at the bottom of the stream. Then "you are no longer pushed or pulled by anything" and "you begin to find your own rest."[6] The deepening of this concentrated state leads to 'the great awakening', to transcendence of our ego and realization of the true nature of our consciousness and all existence. Only then is our 'garden' watered by a soaking rain.

THE CHALLENGE OF TRUE SELF-MASTERY

Meditation and other spiritual practices constitute the means by which kundalini is awakened and the chakras are opened. Nearly all spiritual traditions universally affirm that the discipline of meditation, or interior prayer, is the most effective method by which we can directly penetrate into those interior dimensions of consciousness that underlie and inform our moment-to-moment awareness, but remain hidden underneath layers of unconsciousness. Long-term devotion to daily meditation gradually molds our mind into a powerfully integrated, non- dispersed state. It works very slow and very deep, over many years of relentlessly persistent practice. The constant effort to keep our mind alert and concentrated, sooner or later, demands that we confront and overcome, or transcend, all unconscious compulsive tendencies that cause our attention to remain restless and easily distracted.

Success in concentration requires a degree of self-mastery that is not easy for any of us to achieve, but it opens the door to the spiritual depths of our being. Deep concentration leads ultimately to a state of consciousness in which we transcend the subject-object and conscious-unconscious duality of our mind process, and 'wake up' or become conscious in the boundlessness of the collective, or universal, unconscious. Meditation eventually accomplishes a thorough 'churning' of the ocean of the unconscious, awakening all our latent spiritual potentials.

'CHURNING' THE 'MILKY OCEAN' OF OUR PSYCHE

Meditation both demands and facilitates a tremendous integration of our psyche. Easwaran states unequivocally, "Meditation *is* the integration of consciousness."[7] The relentless pressure to concentrate the distracted energy of our mind and calm its ceaseless waves of activity eventually enable us to gain conscious control over all the compulsive tendencies that drive our thought process. Through long and deep devotion to the practice of meditation, all the diverse energies within our mind are very gradually molded into a powerful, homogenous force consciously focused on penetrating to the heart of life's underlying unity and mystery. Tremendous commitment is required to generate this kind of power, but the psychological freedom and harmony it brings are completely unparalleled.

I am reminded here of one story from the vast world of India's sacred mythology, the 'churning of the milky ocean'. At one point in the early history of the universe, the gods made a truce with their eternal adversaries, the powerful race of demons. Both agreed to cooperate in the great task of churning the cosmic ocean, made of milk, in order to extract from it the elixir of immortality, or *amrita* in Sanskrit, the famous ambrosial liqueur that confers eternal life. Both the gods and demons greatly desired this.

The Indian method of churning uses a piece of wood around which a rope is twisted and pulled back and forth. To churn the cosmic ocean, the serpent *Ananta*, the Endless, is used as the rope coiled around the tall mountain *Mandara*. Slowly with the gods pulling at one end of the great serpent-rope and demons at the other, the mountain is moved back and forth through the infinitely deep milky ocean.

This difficult task requires great perseverance. Were it not for the assistance of *Vishnu*, the Supreme Essence, the gods and demons could not succeed. In addition to other forms of unseen aid, he descends as a great tortoise to the bottom of the ocean to act as an anchor for the *Mandara* mountain as it slowly turns. After a thousand years of churning, various divine creatures and objects rise to the surface, including a milk-white cow and *Airávata*, the heavenly milk-white elephant. First, though, a terrible poison emerges from the cosmic ocean, threatening to destroy the entire operation, until the great god *Shiva* swallows it and neutralizes it by localizing it in his throat, which turns visibly blue from then on. Finally, the goddess *Sri* or *Lakshmi* appears in her celestial form, granting beauty, abundance, and harmony. Then at last the divine physician comes forth bearing a 'moon-cup' filled with the ambrosial nectar, a milk-white bowl made from the crescent moon containing the coveted drink that confers immortality.

THE DYNAMIC TENSION WITHIN OUR PSYCHE CAN BE GRADUALLY RESOLVED

As Chaudhuri and others[8] have pointed out, this myth symbolizes the deep integration and harmonization of the human psyche through long, sustained spiritual practice. The gods and demons are symbolic representations of the fundamental but opposing forces active in the deeper strata of every human consciousness. Gods are the evolutionary energies propelling us toward spiritual development, and demons are the forces of conditioning that retard that development and keep us imprisoned in unconsciousness. The milky ocean is, of course, the psyche and its unknown depths. The gods alone cannot undertake this great task for they have hold of only one end of the psyche's deep energy (*Ananta*, the Endless). The demons have the other end, and the 'churning', which is the practice of meditation, cannot begin in earnest until they cooperate.

This churning, the long devoted practice of meditation, is a labor of integrating our vital energies, our desire and will, and eventually transcending the inherent conscious-unconscious polarity of our psyche. To churn our psyche deeply and thoroughly requires immense persistence, a thousand years, the myth says, before any sign emerges that the *amrita* is forthcoming. But perseverance pays a rich dividend in the end. As our mind becomes homogenized, singular in consistency, undivided, harmonized, and unified, and as the 'poison' of egocentric tendencies is neutralized, our consciousness eventually transcends its narrow personal identity and opens to the unconditioned 'mystery' that is the deeper reality of our being.

In the end, our unified psyche yields up its greatest treasure, the nectar of immortality, the non-dual awareness beyond all opposites, beyond even the boundaries of time and space, of birth and death.

The churning of our psyche through meditation is a back-and-forth motion that gradually facilitates an internal integration of the surface of consciousness, our thinking, perceiving mind, with the deeper causal forces in the unconscious. The continual attempt to calm and focus and transcend our normally restless, dispersed mind creates a dynamic unifying momentum within our psyche. This is the arousing of kundalini. This inward, unifying movement is opposed by the dominant centrifugal force of unconscious conditioning, which is, of course, still pulling for all its worth, trying to keep our psychic energy scattered, unregulated, and projected into all manner of externalized identifications. After long, consistent churning, we begin to sense the undifferentiated, unconditioned energy of pure being that lays deeper than our mind-process and is our true 'home'. The quieter our mind becomes, the more we sense that ocean of spirit, and the more peaceful we become.

For most of us, many hours of energetic meditation practice every day for a long time are necessary to make our mind steady and facilitate the integration of our being. Our spiritual desire must be sufficient to sustain us through years, most likely decades, of hard training with faith in our purpose as our sole support. We will need a deep 'fire' of inspiration burning within to sustain the necessary drive and endurance. The tenacious pull of the world on our mind can gradually be overcome with a continual effort to unify our desires and dedicate ourselves with ever greater resolve to the path of spiritual realization.

DOES MEDITATION BRING ABOUT A REPRESSION OF UNCONSCIOUS CONTENT?

Jung discouraged Westerners from practicing meditation, fearing that it would strengthen the repression of unconscious content, already so submerged and devalued through the modern 'cult' of the rational mind. In his article, 'The Psychology of Eastern Meditation', he explores his reasoning in this regard:

> If a European tries to banish all thought of the outer world and to empty his mind of everything outside, he immediately becomes the prey of his own subjective fantasies . . . Fantasies do not enjoy a good reputation; they are considered cheap and worthless and are therefore rejected as useless and meaningless. They are the *kleshas*, the disorderly and chaotic instinctual forces which yoga proposes to yoke . . . I do not wish to question the possibilities of success when the meditation exercise is conducted in some kind of ecclesiastical setting. But, outside of some such setting, the thing does not as a rule work, or it may even lead to deplorable results. By throwing light on the unconscious one gets first of all into the chaotic sphere of the personal unconscious, which contains all that one would like to forget, and all that one does not wish to admit to oneself or to anybody else, and which one prefers to believe is not true anyhow. One therefore expects to come off best if one looks as little as possible into this dark corner. Naturally, anyone who proceeds

in that way will never get round this corner and will never obtain even a trace of what yoga promises. Only the man who goes through this darkness can hope to make any further progress. I am therefore in principle against the uncritical appropriation of yoga practices by Europeans, because I know only too well that they hope to avoid their own dark corners. Such a beginning is entirely meaningless and worthless.[9]

Kleshas, usually translated as 'afflictions' or 'hindrances', from a root word meaning 'to suffer', were discussed by Jung in the first kundalini yoga seminar. He describes them as root compulsive tendencies that form the basis of human psychic existence. In yoga psychology, the fundamental *klesha* from which all others derive, is nescience, or unconsciousness. From that, ego, the I-sense or sense of personal identity, develops, after which follow attraction to pleasurable or fulfilling experiences, aversion to difficult or painful experiences, and fear of death, the root of all fear. In yoga psychology, these five are the cause of all spiritual and psychological bondage, and must be removed in order to transcend the possibility of suffering.[10]

The times and culture in which Jung formulated his psychology are very different from the 'post-modern' environment in which my own psychological reality has been shaped. Who knows what he might say were he writing now. The concern that he voices here is certainly valid. No significant depth of meditation can be reached until we can corral the energies of the personal unconscious that shape our daily reality and mold them into an integrated force of great dedication and resolve.

But the long-term practice of meditation does not bring about the repression of unconscious content, as it seems Jung feared. In fact, in learning to silence the surface chatter of our mind, many intuitive and creative capacities are greatly enhanced, and life is experienced more synchronistically. The shadowy forces within our mind that drive thought, desire, and imagination must all eventually come under the scrutiny of our deepening power of inner clarity and concentrated vision.

Eventually, if we are able to go very far down this path of inner development, every dark, hidden corner of our psyche can be illumined by the penetrating power of our highly focused inner gaze. This is not repression. Our mind becomes still and deeply concentrated only through the most thorough process of integration, never through repression. Repressed material remains present in the unconscious and will sooner or later surface during meditation, causing a disturbance that begs to be resolved sooner or later.

IF WE WALK SINCERELY ON OUR PATH, WE WILL GROW

Meditation acts as a mirror of the state of our psyche. As Jung recognized, every time we sit with the object of becoming inwardly still, serene, concentrated, and transparent, we come face to face with our conditioning. Our mind has its own agenda of desires, needs, fantasies, concerns, amusements, fears, worries, plans, and so on, *ad infinitum*. The restlessness and distractibility of our mind in meditation is directly proportional to the power exercised by compulsive patterns of conditioning, what Jung calls the shadowy world of the personal unconscious. Only after many years of deep dedication to practice does our mind begin to yield to our insistent resolve to tame it. Even then, there is no easy victory over the mind.

Long-term meditation can only make us stronger, more capable, more fully integrated individuals. It can awaken the deeper spiritual potentials that lay dormant within us, waiting for the right conditions in which to sprout and grow. Yes, there are deep challenges on this path. As Jung said, a 'dabbling' with meditation won't take us too far. But if we walk on this path earnestly and sincerely, no matter how far we go, I do not see how we can avoid some real growth.

I recall my teacher, Baba Hari Dass, saying that one of the most difficult challenges in spiritual development is learning to take 100% responsibility for our progress. There is no God or teacher who will take even one little step for us. Meditation is a slow, safe, thorough, and proven method for integrating our psyche and activating the deepest and greatest potentials of our consciousness. The path is demanding, but all of us whose inner spiritual desire is awakened can walk far on it.

Chapter 5

First Realm: The Call to Awakening

"Awake, Mother! Awake! How long hast thou been asleep in the lotus of the Muladhara! Fulfill thy secret function, Mother: Rise to the thousand-petalled lotus within the head, Where mighty Shiva has his dwelling; swiftly pierce the six lotuses, and take away my grief, O Essence of Consciousness."

SONG TO KUNDALINI, FROM
The Gospel of Sri Ramakrishna

AWAKENING THE FIRE OF SPIRITUAL DESIRE DEEP WITHIN OUR BEING

In kundalini's coiled, deeply conditioned, sleeping state only some of the total energy of our psyche is activated, enough to support the life of our body, senses, and mind, but only in a state of partial consciousness. The symbolism of kundalini yoga, especially of *muladhara*, the base chakra, suggests that deep in the unconscious there is a great reserve of life-energy (*prana*) that is normally untapped. It 'sleeps' there until we are ready to begin the demanding process of spiritual development, which alone can free psychic energy from the grip of our mind's conditioning and open our consciousness to a realization of the unity of all life.

Eknath Easwaran describes this latent energy and the conditions under which it is activated:

> Kundalini is intensely concentrated prana, packed away until we are ready to draw on it. For most human beings this reserve lies hidden and dormant. For kundalini is the fuel we require to complete the long, arduous journey of Self-realization. Until we begin this journey in earnest, to keep us from frittering it away on other pursuits, kundalini cannot be released. But when at last we begin to live for a higher purpose than ourselves, it is as if an intense fire is ignited deep in our consciousness, inflaming our enthusiasm and determination. As we draw on it more and more to make progress, this fire grows until it transfigures our personality.[1]

THE VISUAL REPRESENTATION OF *MULADHARA*, THE 'ROOT' CHAKRA

Located anatomically at the base of the spine in the area of the perineum, this psychic center is clearly the 'ground floor' of the seven-tiered structure of spiritual development. It is the state of consciousness in which our spiritual development begins, and from which the latent kundalini power, or evolutionary energy hidden within the unconscious, begins to awaken and ascend to the higher chakras. To understand *muladhara*, which literally means 'root support', is the key to unlocking the whole symbolism of the chakras and kundalini yoga.

Muladhara chakra is visually represented as a four-petaled lotus within which is a large square.[2] The petals are vermilion in color, and the square is yellow, the color of earth, for this is the earth realm. In the center of the square is a small triangle, a symbol of the *yoni*, the female sexual organ. In the vast symbolic and mythological world of Indian spirituality, this sacred symbol represents creation, or the creative power of Nature. It is closely connected to the Sanskrit word *shakti*, the divine creative energy of the universe, which is characterized as feminine, as kundalini is also.

The apex of this small triangle points downward, indicating that the flow of creative life energy is down and out into the manifest world. Within the triangle is a *lingam*, often depicted as an erect stone, a phallic symbol associated with the god Shiva and representing spiritual reality as fully transcendent, as uncreated, unchanging, and absolute. This *lingam* is said to be *svayambhu*, 'self-born' or existing in its own right with dependence on nothing outside itself. Although a very different kind of symbol than we Westerners are accustomed to, this is the equivalent in Judeo-Christian tradition of 'God, the Father' or Jesus' designation, 'the Father within'.

The kundalini serpent is coiled around the *lingam* three-and-one/half times. Its raised head points downward, and its mouth covers the opening to the narrow channel called *sushumna* that extends from the top of the *lingam* up through the entire chakra and out the very tip of the upper lotus petal. It is this channel that connects the chakras together. A large gray elephant, the most heavy, solid, and 'earthy' of animals, is located below the triangle.

THE SYMBOLISM OF *MULADHARA* CHAKRA

This visual image is a symbolic picture of the human psyche in its normal state, tied to the earth realm. Here we experience ourselves as separate embodied persons trying to make sense out of our lives in a diverse world of many beings, objects, forces, and so on, both known and unknown. Our consciousness is 'boxed in', circumscribed by the fixed limits of the human mind or ego, beyond which we cannot venture. All our psychic energy is directed 'earth-ward', out into the manifest world of the senses, the world of appearances. Even our creative imagination is tied to images based on sensory awareness.

But hidden deep within the heart of our psyche is kundalini, the potential for perfect peace, for the full conscious realization of our life and all life as infinite. The kundalini serpent is sleeping. The spiritual capacity within us, our amazing capacity to penetrate deep into our own inner reality and come to know ourselves as pure and eternal and all-embracing, is dormant, fast asleep, a seed yet to sprout. Entry into the path of consciousness-development that leads into and through the interior dimensions of our psyche, is closed off in this state.

The sleeping kundalini 'dreams' the world into existence. In *muladhara* kundalini is the 'world-bewilderer', the creative, projecting power deep within the unconscious that dazzles us with the senses and all they perceive, but keeps us in spiritual darkness, unaware of our true nature as unconditioned and free of all limitation. Kundalini is sometimes known as *maya-shakti*, the creative energy of the universe and the human psyche, that spins out the world of *namarupa*, of 'name and form', the visible everyday realm of matter, senses, and mind.

According to the yoga tradition, there are two psychic forces at work as kundalini slumbers. The first is 'veiling', limiting our awareness to its ego or mind manifestation while covering the spiritual truth upon which our whole being rests with a thick cloud of unconsciousness. The second force at work is 'projecting' or dazzling our limited personal awareness with a ceaseless stream (except in the state of deep dreamless sleep) of images, perceptions, sensations, thoughts, feelings, experiences, and so on. This stream of consciousness is experienced as immediate psychic reality, as our 'self' and as the 'real' world.

JUNG AT HIS BEST IN EXPLAINING THE ROOT CHAKRA

In explaining his view of *muladhara* chakra, Jung was at his best. His comments touch on many important points. He begins by noting that *muladhara* is located anatomically in the area of the perineum, but it is not, as we might guess, a region "having to do with sexuality and all sorts of unsavory things" He describes his idea of the base chakra as a stage of development in which the ego or mind is conscious, but the true self is asleep:

> And in which stage is the self asleep and the ego conscious? *Here*, of course, in this conscious world where we are all reasonable and respectable people, adapted individuals as one says. Everything runs smoothly; we are going to have lunch, we have appointments, we are perfectly normal citizens of certain states. We are under certain obligations and cannot run away easily without getting neurotic; we have to look after our duties. So we are all in the roots, we are upon our root support. We are in our roots right in this world—when you buy your ticket from the streetcar conductor, for instance, or for the theater,

or pay the waiter—that is reality as you touch it. And then the self is asleep, which means that all things concerning the gods are asleep.

ENTANGLED IN EARTHLY CAUSALITIES

Jung paints a vivid picture of the 'world' of *muladhara* as being the normal state of consciousness in which this very concrete, practical, day-to-day world we all live in is implicitly accepted as the 'real' world. He says that the root chakra is a symbol of "our present psychic situation, because we live entangled in earthly causalities." He is careful to note that *muladhara* does not just symbolize the manifest world in which we all live, but that it represents our psychic condition, our whole interior and exterior consciousness in our normal daily life in the world. In our consciousness of everyday life, he says, "we are like highly developed animals, tied down by our environment and entangled and conditioned by it."

But, of course, we don't view life that way in modern Western culture. Rather, we tend to consider ourselves quite evolved, the 'lords of nature' as Jung called us. We sit above all lower forms of life, and cultivate our power over nature and life, for purposes both desirable and undesirable. In some respects, we are like human gods, masters of our destiny.

In the psychic state symbolized by *muladhara*, where the concerns of life revolve around our bodies, relationships, careers, families, enjoyment, and activities in the world, we do have a certain ability to choose our path in life. But our choices are far more limited than we tend to realize. Our awareness is heavily conditioned by interior and exterior forces that are not within our conscious control. Our bodies are subject to the laws of nature, to the cycle of birth/growth/decay/death. As embodied beings we cannot escape the limitations and conditions imposed by natural law, any more than a goat or chicken can escape the life that nature has given it.

Our minds are also subject to massive conditioning, nearly all of which is unconscious and not easy to access. Below the surface of our awareness lay the vast and unknown world of the unconscious, from which every thought, feeling, and act arises. Although perfectly normal and well adapted to society, as long as our personal life in the world is what is 'real' to us, we are living surrounded and imprisoned by our own unconsciousness. Of course, we don't realize that, nor do we care to. Nonetheless, this is the psychic situation that we all find ourselves in to begin with.

"ONLY A LITTLE MORE FREE THAN THE HIGHER ANIMALS"

At the beginning of the fourth and final seminar session in Jung's 1932 series, one of the participants asked a very important question: "I do not understand why our daily life should be thought of as taking place solely in *muladhara*. Would not *muladhara* apply more to the life of animals and primitives who live in complete harmony with nature?" Jung used almost the entire session in a brilliant response to this question. After expounding the symbolic nature of the chakra system, which views the totality of the human psyche, not just the conscious mind, he says:

> It is as if we viewed our psychology and the psychology of mankind from the standpoint of a fourth dimension, unlimited by space or time. The cakra system is created from this standpoint. It is a standpoint that transcends time and the individual. . . .

Only when we have become acquainted with the wide extent of the psyche, and no longer remain inside the confines of the conscious alone, can we know that our consciousness is entangled in *muladhara*....

It is as if a superconsciousness, an all-embracing divine consciousness, surveyed the psyche from above. Looked at from the angle of this four-dimensional consciousness, we can recognize the fact that we are still living in *muladhara*.... In the state of ordinary consciousness, we are actually down below, entangled, rooted in the earth under a spell of illusions, dependent—in short, only a little more free than the higher animals. We have culture, it is true, but our culture is not suprapersonal; it is culture in *muladhara*....

Nonetheless, we do not know that we are in *muladhara*.... Our culture represents the conscious held prisoner in *muladhara*.

A DARING JOURNEY INTO THE UNKNOWN

What we generally think of as healthy personal development, although no doubt important to a satisfying life in the world, is no development at all from the viewpoint of the chakras. The awakening of kundalini represents a completely different kind of developmental process, being the exploration and integration of our vast, unknown psyche as a whole, rather than just the pursuit of personal fulfillment in the context of this world. Only the outermost realms of our being are personal in nature.

The true depth and substance of our being is universal and spiritual in nature, even though we are normally unconscious at these levels. Our personal self, which is all we know, must be left behind on our journey to discover the truth of who we are. We must find a way to enter into the unknown, the deep mystery of our being that has nothing to do with our personal life and sense of self. That is why spiritual development requires a rare kind of daring, courage, and passion.

Regardless how developed in intelligence and worldly capacities our personal or cultural consciousness may be, until we awaken to another deeper kind of development, the unification of the psyche as a whole, we are mired in the realm of 'earthly causalities', asleep to the spiritual reality underlying our very identity and existence.

'PSYCHIC SLEEP'

Although we can never be separated from the universal, spiritual foundations of our being, we have virtually no awareness of our psyche beyond our conscious mind. We may think of ourselves as the 'masters' of this world, but from the standpoint of depth psychology, we are really slaves to our conditioning. We may be able to manipulate matter in rather dazzling fashion, but we are infants in exploring the nature of our own consciousness.

Jung says bluntly, and accurately: "*Muladhara* is a condition of psychic sleep." The 'gods' are asleep, he claimed. We are conscious at the body and mind level, but the non-egoic, spiritual potentials that represent our true destiny as conscious beings, are present within us only as unsprouted seeds still buried in the unconscious. There is no awareness of the spiritual core of our being and no movement toward its realization. The unknown depths of consciousness may be projected into a God-idea or other ideas or symbols that we conceive of as external to ourselves, but they remain completely unrealized as our very truth and reality.

ೞ

THE OUTER COURTYARD IS A STATE OF EXILE

Various metaphors of sleep, darkness, imprisonment, drunkenness, slavery, sin, a 'fallen' state, and so forth, are universally used to represent the condition of normal egocentric consciousness from a spiritual perspective. Teresa describes it as 'this exile'. She means, of course, the state of separation from God, a state in which our being is polarized into a conscious mind that is exiled from, or completely unaware of, its true source and substance, the 'Inner Ruler' of the castle who remains hidden within many levels of interiority. This deep interior presence, the source of all light, all consciousness, cannot be known because it transcends our mind's cognitive capacities. Our mind is limited to seeing material and mental objects and cannot comprehend the greater unity of the whole psyche in which the duality of subject and object, knower and known, is dissolved.

This state of exile, or polarization of our psyche into conscious and unconscious, can be, and often is, very pronounced. Then such a dark cloud of unconsciousness, in Teresa's words, a 'black cloth', separates our mind from the spiritual roots of consciousness, that we begin to think our ego or personal conscious self is the only king of this castle. Such a condition can very quickly and easily lead to the state of what Teresa calls 'mortal sin'. Our mind is so divorced from the soul, or depths of consciousness, that we are motivated only by narrow self-interest.

EVEN IN 'GOOD TIMES' WE CANNOT ESCAPE FEAR, ANXIETY, AND MENTAL DISPERSION

This is, in fact, our human condition. We all begin in this state of partial consciousness: the ego or personal mind is conscious, but the psyche as a whole remains lost in the darkness of primal unconsciousness. As civilized as we modern people are, we are still living in psychological and spiritual unconsciousness. We don't have to look far for the proof: fear, anger, confusion, blame, violence, greed, distrust, insecurity, alienation, and so on. All these and more are the product of our unconsciousness. A universal fear and anxiety lay at the very bottom of our human mind.

"But," you may say, "I am happy, and I do good things in the world. I cherish my personal life, my relationships, my work, my religion, my pleasures. What is all this talk of darkness and unconsciousness?" Even though we may, for a time, be satisfied with our lives and attempting to create a meaningful and fulfilling life within our societal context, if we explore the interior world of our motivations, we will discover that unconscious forces are shaping our entire existence. If tragedy or death comes unannounced, our lives can be thrown into turmoil, and our minds into depression. If we lose all our financial security, we can become consumed by worry and fear. And if we try to meditate sincerely, we will discover that our minds are almost completely out of our conscious control.

Realization of the 'Inner Sun', the hidden source of infinite life and consciousness deep within us, can hardly be imagined when all we know is body, senses, mind, and world. Our psychic energy is unconsciously projected into a confusing diversity of desires, thoughts, feelings, and so on. Its force or power is dispersed, consumed in innumerable channels of psychic activity. Teresa laments the state of such a soul:

> How sad a thing it is to see a soul separated from this light! How miserable is the state of those poor

rooms within the castle! How disturbed the senses are, that is, the people who live in these rooms! And in the faculties, that is among the custodians, the stewards, and the chief waiters, what blindness, what bad management!

A SHADOWY WORLD OF WILD AND DANGEROUS CREATURES

From a spiritual perspective, Teresa's image of the outer courtyard is a place of only a little dim light. She portrays a shadowy world full of wild and dangerous creatures, symbols for the compulsive tendencies within our consciousness that increase our sense of separateness and deepen our condition of 'exile'. This civilized world is still quite brutish, and it is nothing more than the 'mirrored' externalization of our collective human mind.

Those living in the outer courtyard, Teresa says, are like persons that do not know who their mother or father is, or from what country they come:

> Wouldn't it show great ignorance, my daughters, if someone when asked who he was didn't know, and didn't know his father or mother or from what country he came? Well now, if this would be so extremely stupid, we are incomparably more so when we do not strive to know who we are, but limit ourselves to considering only roughly these bodies. Because we have heard and because faith tells us so, we know we have souls. But we seldom consider the precious things that can be found in this soul, or who dwells within it, or its high value. Consequently, little effort is made to preserve its beauty. All our attention is taken up with the plainness of the diamond's setting or the outer wall of the castle; that is, with these bodies of ours.

☙

In the outer courtyard we are living on the surface of consciousness, 'exiled' from the center of our being, living from a script we didn't write, having no conception of "the sublime dignity and beauty of the soul", which is beyond our intellect's power of comprehension. Unaware of our dangerous predicament, we become so accustomed to living in the dim light with all our projected fears, worries, judgments, and so on, that our lives are in danger of losing that true spiritual dignity and beauty that is rightfully ours. We have no awareness of our spiritual source and the true nature of our being. Without even knowing it, we are the victims of compulsive tendencies that govern all the activities of our body and mind.

Teresa offers a stinging psychological commentary: our human awareness, she says, can become so deeply and compulsively mired in its own egocentricity that we carry on 'like brute beasts'. Of course, animals are somewhat more innocent in their native bestiality, but humans are not. We carry our sins, the karmic fruit of our unconscious acts and intentions, around our necks like a great burden. Teresa uses reptiles as symbols of the power of instinctual forces in our consciousness. Without psychological and spiritual development, she warns us, we are in danger of remaining trapped in the instinctual level of consciousness that we all inherit as embodied creatures.

THE 'I-MAKER' OR 'EGO' FUNCTION IN OUR CONSCIOUSNESS

The nature of our consciousness is indeed like that of a clear crystal, because it takes on the color or quality of that with which it becomes associated. In the presence of heat, we say, "I am hot." In the presence of danger, "I am afraid." When experiencing strong sexual desire, "I am enflamed," and so on. We all normally become identified with whatever experience our body/mind is having, as of course we would when we are conscious only as body, mind, and personal self.

This fundamental tendency in our consciousness to be identified with what our body/mind is perceiving or experiencing, is called *ahamkara* in the yoga tradition, which literally means 'I-maker'. Depth psychology calls it the 'ego' function. All human beings naturally take on a sense of personal identity in this way, until and unless we grow beyond it through a difficult but very rewarding journey of true psychological and spiritual development.

Jung characterized *muladhara* as that place where "man is bound to the world of appearance and believes that his ego is identical with his self." By self, he means our true self, the depth and unity of our whole psyche. Indeed, this is the identifying characteristic of *muladhara* and the outer courtyard of the castle: our conscious mind is implicitly accepted as the whole of psychic reality. It is as if the waves on the surface of the ocean (of consciousness) believe they are the whole of the ocean because they have no experience of the great depth that lay beneath them.

"WE ARE NON-INDIVIDUAL—WE ARE JUST FISH IN THE SEA"

The autonomy of our individual life is far more apparent than real. We are victims of hidden forces that, for the most part, we neither recognize nor control. Even though our lives may appear to be meaningful to us, we are, as Jung said, 'just fish in the sea'. We have not yet become 'individuated'. We have yet to grow into our true individuality, our true destiny and potential as individual beings. To do so requires a most courageous journey of consciousness development.

CB

The development of personal identity in the world, regardless how positive or substantial it seems, does not make us real, or complete, individuals, although we may believe that it does. Modern culture is accustomed to thinking of individuality in the shallow sense of differing personal qualities, interests, and accomplishments. But these only serve to distinguish persons from each other, as one fish is distinguished from another.

Only as we awaken to the deep inner longing to discover the source and essence of our being, do we embark on a journey that will require us to give all that we are, and in turn will give birth to all that we can be as self-aware beings. True individuality is born to the extent that all grasping after personal identity is left behind on the daring journey to conscious realization of the deep mystery of our being.

At the beginning of our spiritual journey, we are still just another fish in the human sea. While living in the outer courtyard of our being, awake to body, mind, and our personal life in the world, we cannot know the infinite depth and wholeness of our being any more than a fish can know what lay outside the sea in which it lives.

PLATO'S 'CAVE ANALOGY'

In his famous 'cave analogy' Plato paints a vivid picture of the state of consciousness symbolized by *muladhara* and the outer courtyard of the interior castle. Imagine, he says, sitting in a dark underground cave, facing the back wall, with a small opening behind and far above that lets in just a little light. Having been chained to this spot since birth, and therefore unaware of the source of this light, we see only shadows dancing on the cave wall, believing them to be absolutely real and substantial because we have no idea any other reality exists.

Now if one person is somehow freed from his chains, and turning toward the source of light, is dazzled, but eventually manages the 'steep and rugged ascent' up through the small opening and out into the full light of the Sun, he would then know for certain that what he had previously took to be the real world while in the cave, was only a world of shadows, an incessant movie-like stream of insubstantial images projected on to the screen of the cave wall.

So it is that in our normal human state of mind-bound consciousness, the convincing reality of the sense-world dominates our consciousness and circumscribes its vision, its 'dwelling place'. It is all we know, it is the house we live in, and seems so very real and substantive. The depth dimension of consciousness, home of our true Being, the spiritual reality that is the substance of our life and all life, seems like a distant idea, a mere abstraction created by the fertile human imagination.

THE CALL TO 'WAKE UP' FROM OUR ANCIENT SLUMBER

The symbolism of *muladhara* chakra and the outer courtyard of *Interior Castle* points toward the great danger of 'sleepwalking' through life, unaware of the spiritual reality that lays behind our individual consciousness. To the extent that our awareness is unconsciously identified only with the senses and the mind, to that extent are we asleep to the truth of our being. Thus, in all traditions there are exhortations to wake up and realize our true nature.

When we are ready to hear it, this 'call to awakening' comes forth into our awareness from the unknown interior depths of our being. We are forever drawn back to those depths, the source of our being. In each of us, this call may manifest a little differently but will always be experienced sooner or later as an inner longing for peace, freedom, wholeness, lasting fulfillment, a kind of 'remembering' or intuition of a state of psychic unity.

Once this call to awakening surfaces, it will not leave us alone until we respond to it. The 'divine fisherman' has hooked us. We may thrash around for a very long time, but we cannot escape. The time has come for us to undertake the journey we are destined for, the journey that will unify our being and fulfill the promise of our human birth, the journey into the very innermost secret center of our being.

A DEEP 'REMEMBERING'

Inscribed in our heart of hearts, in the depths of our awareness, is the 'memory' of our true identity as spiritual beings, 'made in the image of God', never born, never dying. From deep within us comes this call, awakening us to a new life of inner seeking, inspiring us to undertake the difficult journey back to our source and essence, and leading us toward a wholeness that we know will satisfy our deepest longing.

In the wonderful Gnostic allegory called "The Hymn of the Pearl,"[3] the prince who has forgotten his royal birth and his real identity, living now in bondage to the sense world, receives a 'letter' of awakening from his parents, the 'King of Kings' and the 'Mistress of the East'. "Awake and arise from your sleep, and hear the words of our letter." It reminds him of his royal stature and of his great mission: to recover the "one pearl, which is in the midst of the sea, in the abode of the loud-breathing serpent" and return home with it so that he may become "heir in our kingdom."

The prince awakens from his sleep of unconsciousness, hastens to steal the pearl from the fearsome dragon and begin the journey to his home in the East. The letter flies like an eagle before him, guiding and inspiring him on his way. He says: "And according to what was traced on my heart, so was the letter written. I remembered that I was a son of Kings, and my soul yearned for its noble state."

THE SPROUTING OF THE EVOLUTIONARY SEED OF CONSCIOUSNESS DEVELOPMENT

Out of the soil of our life experience in this world, the 'germ' of spiritual desire can sprout, propelling us on a journey toward the eternal, far beyond the limits of our personal identity. Our personal consciousness is the 'earth' in which the 'seed' of spiritual realization or complete consciousness is buried, dormant, waiting for the right time and conditions in our individual psyche to sprout. Buried far beneath the surface of our thinking, perceiving mind lays the potential for unified consciousness, consciousness free of all conditioning. Kundalini is the energy within our psyche by which this seed sprouts and grows. Chakras and the dwelling places within our 'interior castle' represent the stages of its growth and development.

All human beings experience within themselves a deep longing for wholeness and real fulfillment, for an end to the fragmentation of our psyche and the dispersion of its core energy. Sooner or later, this inner longing asserts itself, and we begin to make some deliberate move toward greater self-awareness and psychic integration. Then we can say that we see the door of the interior castle and are thinking of opening it.

Teresa is clear that the door through which we enter into ourselves, into our spiritual depth, is prayer and meditation. In our modern age with its popularization of psychology, it is true that a certain degree of 'inner work' can be undertaken through therapeutic and related methods that are not based on a commitment to meditation and spiritual practice. All such work can, of course, be valuable for individual development. And we can build psychological 'muscles' that will be indispensable when we undertake the daunting task of unifying and illuminating our whole being, conscious and unconscious.

But the stirring of kundalini, the spiritual energy of consciousness, is more than just a need or desire to explore the inner world of our personal psychological conditioning. It is experienced as a longing for realization of that core mystery in which we have our being, a desire to know ourselves as 'spirits free and blessed', a 'fire' deep in our consciousness that drives us to seek the wholeness of spiritual realization.

To enter into the first dwelling places of the castle of the psyche is to be touched by this fire and to begin to feed it through a commitment to spiritual practice. The spark of kundalini or true spiritual desire must be ignited deep within us. Just how this happens can vary from person to person, but happen it must. Even though it may be small and deeply buried, we will feel this inner fire burning once it is truly ignited. We will not be able to ignore it.

Very often this inner fire is sparked by association with a realized spiritual teacher, one who communicates by example the potential for true peace and freedom. It can also happen by other means. When we are psychologically ready to grasp the possibility of awakening and sense that our destiny lay in following this call, this inner spiritual fire will be ignited. The unconscious knows when we are ready. It is kundalini stirring from her ancient slumber in the lotus of *muladhara*.

A 'ROCK-SOLID' COMMITMENT TO DAILY SPIRITUAL PRACTICE

The first rooms within the interior castle lay still within the world of *muladhara*. In each chakra, a significant development of consciousness must take place in order to be ready to prepare us to go deeper into our being and 'open' the next chakra. What Teresa calls the first dwelling place represents the development necessary within *muladhara* to prepare us to enter the second chakra.

At the beginning of spiritual development, the key to progress is acquiring an unassailable, rock-solid commitment to daily spiritual practice. Daily meditation, or interior prayer as it may sometimes be called, is the bedrock of spiritual life. Over many years the regularity of practice will begin to weaken the conditioned tendencies that give rise to the restlessness of our mind. Ever so slowly our mind will come under the control of our unified life-purpose. As we persist in the practice of meditation and other spiritual disciplines, we begin to 'take hold of our consciousness'.

During this first stage, our spiritual desire gradually grows stronger, more insistent. It begins to act as a unifying force within our psyche, providing a sense of purpose, hope, and groundedness in a vision of reality beyond the limitations of the separate self. No great peace descends on us here, only a slow infusion of new and deeper meaning, an awareness of life as offering both a greater challenge and a greater fulfillment than we previously imagined. So begins the energization and spiritualization of our being that will eventually lead to the complete realization of its deepest truth.

SELF-KNOWLEDGE AND HUMILITY

Teresa discusses two essential qualities that spiritual practice must embody at the beginning of our journey of inner development: self-knowledge and inspiration. By self-knowledge, she means an awareness of our own nothingness in relation to God, the true reality of our being. She refers to the first dwelling place as the rooms where humility is acquired:

> I do not know if this has been explained well. Knowing ourselves is something so important that I wouldn't want any relaxation ever in this regard, however high you may have climbed into the heavens. While we are on this earth nothing is more important to us than humility.... In my opinion we shall never completely know ourselves if we don't strive to know God. By gazing at His grandeur, we get in touch with our own lowliness; by looking at His purity, we shall see our own filth; by pondering His humility, we shall see how far we are from being humble.

Understood psychologically, Teresa's insistence on self-knowledge represents a growing recognition of our mind's total dependence on a deeper unconscious source for its very life and sustenance. We become keenly aware that we are not the master of our own house. Soon after we take up the practice of meditation we begin to see how uncontrolled our minds really are. The more truly we see this, the more humility we gain. We cannot, regardless how hard we try, discover the origin of our mind's energy. We begin to sense the mysterious depth of our being, and an intimation of spiritual freedom, or peace beyond understanding, gradually dawns within us.

The humility born of self-knowledge is the foundation of spiritual development. If I have learned one thing in my years of spiritual practice, it is that my thinking/perceiving mind is nothing in itself. All its seeming power and intelligence comes from an interior source that it does not recognize. Indeed, our conscious mind—with its desires, attachments, likes and dislikes, fears, opinions, and especially its ever-present sense of self-importance—is the playground of devils, the field in which unconscious forces express themselves and sport with human life. They are powerful enemies, and there is wisdom in giving them total respect.

AVOIDING THE 'WILES' OF THE DEVIL

Teresa comments that our challenge in this first stage is to avoid the 'wiles' of the devil, the power of unconsciousness, to deceive us and prevent our further progress:

> I could give some very good proofs from experience of the wiles the devil uses in these first dwelling places. Thus I say that you should think not in terms of just a few rooms but in terms of a million; for souls, all with good intentions enter here in many ways. But since the devil always has such a bad intention, he must have in each room many legions of devils to fight off souls when they try to go from one room to the other. Since the poor soul doesn't know this, the devil plays tricks on it in a thousand ways. He's not so successful with those who have advanced closer to where the King dwells. But since in the first rooms souls are still absorbed in the world and engulfed in their pleasures and vanities, with their honors and

pretenses, their vassals (which are these senses and faculties) don't have the strength God gave human nature in the beginning. And these souls are easily conquered, even though they may go about with desires not to offend God and though they do perform good works.

Unconscious forces within us are extremely hidden and subtle, so they are difficult for us be aware of and to overcome. Gradually we have to learn to exercise great vigilance to weaken them and to grow more conscious. They are our enemy as we walk down the path of spiritual development. A prime example is the struggle we often experience as we begin this path to commit to a serious daily meditation practice. This very well may mean having to wake up and get out of bed earlier every day than we would like. We may have to fight a very tough battle to establish a solid 1½ or 2 hour daily practice period before we begin our day's activities. Only when our inner spiritual fire is burning vigorously will we acquire the necessary motivation to do this.

WE NEED A FIRE OF INSPIRATION

Teresa points out that the work of self-knowledge must be balanced by that of inspiration. Lacking a vision of our spiritual nature, and a burning desire to realize it, we may struggle to find the courage, daring, and resolve that will be required for us to move toward the more interior realms of consciousness. We must be fired with sustained enthusiasm in order to progress further into our own nature. Truly has it been said, in regard to the demands of inner work, that "no effort can be consistently put in by anyone unless he has seen an inspiring goal."[4]

All progress at this point is made through our own motivation and persistent effort. The key to success is continuous and intense inspiration. Somehow, that inspiration has to be awakened in us and fed on a daily basis. Association with true spiritual teachers and communities of seekers is very helpful. Daily spiritual reading of works written by men and women of true realization is almost a necessity. We have to begin to eat, sleep, and breathe with this idea of spiritual development.

Often we feel inspired and excited at the beginning of our spiritual journey. After awhile, though, we see that progress does not come quickly or easily. Well may our inspiration wane after this initial 'high' wears off, and we become aware of the commitment to long years of hard work that are necessary to make any significant progress. In order for spiritual practice to bear fruit, we must be 'driven' by an inner longing that is powerful enough to overcome the many forces that will resist the development of consciousness, not the least of which is the desire to live a comfortable, safe, and 'normal' existence in society.

We will need to awaken a deeper, hotter fire of life-energy and life-purpose than that. The further we go, the greater our fire of inspiration and dedication must be. Even in this first stage, we will face serious tests of our commitment and the depth of our desire to walk on this path. The pressures and allurements of modern life present innumerable opportunities to be distracted from our purpose. If our motivation is too weak, we will, as Teresa points out, easily fall prey to the power of unconscious tendencies that pull our mind into the 'hurly-burly' of life in the world, and into a state of confusion and dispersion that lacks the strength and clarity required to move forward.

☙

THE DAWNING OF A DEEP UNIVERSAL LIFE-PURPOSE

But as long as a spark of true spiritual desire is awakened in us, we are on our path and will move forward. If we are sincere in our desire to grow spiritually and apply ourselves, we will gradually find our way. Once we make some progress, it is ours to keep. Yes, we can backslide, but our unconscious will 'remember' our progress and at the right time coax us into further growth. The development of our 'consciousness potentials' is really all we have in this life, and all that we have to give. And that can be a powerful source of motivation for us: to give to ourselves, to those we love, to a world that sorely needs a growth in consciousness.

Our spiritual desire is personal at first, but grows more universal as it deepens. We work for our own freedom because we want freedom for all. The more universal our life-purpose becomes, the more personal sacrifice we are willing to make to fulfill it. It is a great blessing to be on our path of spiritual development.

Chapter 6

Second Realm: The Battlefield of the Personal Unconscious

"When you become a traveler on the path to your Inner Being, the distance that separates you from your Goal gradually vanishes. You will most certainly have to undertake this pilgrimage to immortality, trampling underfoot hundreds and hundreds of obstacles and impediments. This is the kind of courage that has to be awakened."

SRI ANANDAMAYI MA, A 20TH-CENTURY
WOMAN SAINT FROM NORTH INDIA

RE-DIRECTING OUR LIFE ENERGY INWARD

In *muladhara* the mouth of the kundalini serpent faces downward, covering the entrance to *sushumna*, the secret channel to the deep center of our being. To reach the second chakra, kundalini must do a 180-degree turn, enter *sushumna*, and begin to uncoil. In *muladhara*, our psychic energy is projected outward, into the manifest world or into an imagination rooted in the images of that world. Such is our native human condition. When we hear the call to awakening, we begin to redirect our conscious energy inward, toward the invisible depths of our being, out of which we mysteriously seem to emerge.

The turning of the kundalini serpent from downward-facing to upward-facing occurs as the force of our desire, our life-energy, is redirected toward spiritual striving, toward the search for wholeness, peace, freedom, and limitless capacity to give. We do not necessarily give up external pursuits, but gradually learn to engage in them in a manner that supports our inner development and weakens the conditioning that keeps us spiritually 'unconscious'.

SVADHISTHANA, THE WATERY REALM OF THE PERSONAL UNCONSCIOUS

When the inward/upward flow of our psychic energy gains momentum we reach *svadhisthana*, the second chakra, a six-petaled lotus anatomically located in the spinal column just above and behind the sexual organs. *Svadhisthana* means 'dwelling-place of the self' and is characterized as a 'white shining watery region' in the shape of a half-moon. Here in the waters live powerful sea creatures and a variety of demons, symbols of the powerful forces of instinct and conditioning that live in the 'sea of the unconscious'. The solidity of the square earth realm dissolves into the more subtle fluidity of the lunar water realm. The animal symbol of *svadhisthana* is the *makara*, a mythical creature like an alligator or crocodile, or alternately, a sea monster. It is pictured with its mouth open.

Each higher chakra represents a more subtle, hidden, and less differentiated world within our human psyche. In *muladhara* our psychic reality is fully externalized and experienced in the concrete forms of body, self, and world. Just beneath the surface of our normal awareness lay a submerged realm of conditioning that is the immediate source of all our thoughts, feelings, sensations, and so on. This is the water realm.

Our stream of consciousness, quiet only during deep dreamless sleep, is generated by these unconscious forces that make their home below the threshold of our awareness. In depth psychology, this realm is generally called the personal unconscious. Even though we are in a world of unconscious forces and tendencies here, they are still personal in nature. These forces have their roots in a deeper, collective strata of our psyche, but in this realm they are closer to the surface of our awareness and are shaping it in a way that varies somewhat from person to person.

"THE SEAT OF ERROR AND DESIRE"

In this realm our psyche's core energy resides, 'coiled up' in the form of instinct, sexuality, and conditioned tendencies. Here our consciousness is molded and shaped before flowing outward into the visible form apprehended by our mind. Just as water takes the course of least resistance, the energy of our mind flows through the channels of conditioned desires, needs, fears, and so on, which are most deeply carved in our unconscious.

In his kundalini yoga seminars, Jung claimed that *svadhisthana* "must be the unconscious, symbolized by the sea. We may assume that the way out of our *muladhara* existence leads into the water." He equated the *makara* with the Biblical leviathan, a dangerous sea-monster capable of devouring people. The encounter with the unconscious, according to Jung, is a baptismal initiation that carries with it the very real danger of being swallowed by this monster of the deep. We may be overwhelmed by the power of unconscious forces that are released when, through one means or another, we open ourselves to their reality and influence. Alcohol, drugs, stress, fear, and other conditions can open this door so suddenly and so wide that the danger of being overwhelmed by the unconscious is very great.

Jung called *svadhisthana* "the seat of error and desire," presumably because of the inescapable tendency in all of us to become the victim of our conditioning. Whether expressed as a struggle with devils or demons, or as the 'night sea journey' in which we must wrestle with the great monster of the deep, this battle with the interior forces that shape our personal reality must be undertaken in earnest by all of us who aspire toward realization of the deeper reality of our being.

A WHOLE WORLD OF INTERIOR FORCES

At this stage, upon entering the second chakra or dwelling place within the interior structure of our psyche, we encounter a whole 'world' of conditioned forces, habitual tendencies, and instinctual drives. They mold our individual personality and generate our moment-to-moment experience. If we succeed in winning the many battles that take place here and gradually gain control over this realm, then we can move deeper into our psyche, into the more universal roots of our consciousness. But for now the battle rages in this realm of the personal unconscious where an impressive array of submerged forces give rise to the stream of images, feelings, sensations, thoughts, desires, and so on, that constitute our awareness.

A GROWING DETERMINATION TO WALK ON THIS PATH, HARD THOUGH IT BE

As we work our way far into these second dwelling places we must sooner or later taste the bittersweet quality of our striving. Spiritual desire now grips our mind with far greater force and insistence, and we feel infused with a new depth of energy and purpose. And we also are beginning to see that to fulfill our spiritual destiny means fighting and winning a great battle. We have come far enough now on our path to realize how hard it is to turn the energy of our consciousness, our attention and desires and will, away from the visible world, which is all we know, and re-direct it toward realization of the invisible Mystery far within our being.

We intuitively sense that this Mystery is our deepest truth, but we also begin to sense how long the journey may be to consciously reach It. Yet now we are determined to walk forward as best we can, even if the gate is narrow and the path hard, for we are driven by a relentless, inner urge to 'go home', to return to our original, unconditioned state of wholeness and freedom.

Teresa says about the second dwelling places: "These rooms, in part, involve much more effort than do the first, even though there is not as much danger, for it now seems that souls in them recognize the dangers, and there is great hope they will enter further into the castle." The inner call to awakening is now loud and clear and comes often into our consciousness. But, Teresa points out, we can make no direct response at this point, for we have not yet learned to 'speak', to answer the 'Lord's call', by a direct realization of the spiritual depths of our being.

We suffer more than in the first rooms, Teresa says, because we are so acutely attuned to this inner longing, yet feel frustrated by our inability to fulfill it. But she reminds us, "after all it is a wonderful thing to hear what is being said to us," and we can take solace in the knowledge that "His Majesty knows well how to wait many days and years, especially when He sees perseverance and good desires. This perseverance is most necessary here."

**DEEP INNER CERTAINTY ABOUT
OUR LIFE PURPOSE**

Now we have reached an inner certainty regarding our life purpose. We have undertaken serious spiritual practice and feel increasingly determined to face the many challenges encountered in the process of purifying or de-conditioning our minds and developing our consciousness-potential. Reaching this deep, full sense of clarity about our life-path is no small accomplishment, given the pervasive influence of societal values that invariably tend to pull us into many externalized and dispersed desires. Until we become established in this inner certainty, it is nearly impossible to make the depth of commitment necessary to move forward. This is not a place for dabbling in spirituality.

SPIRITUAL PRACTICE BECOMES THE 'BEDROCK' OF OUR LIFE

Teresa advises those who are entering the second stage of spiritual development "to strive to give up unnecessary things and business affairs" to the extent that their position in life permits. "It is something so important in order for him to reach the main dwelling places that if he doesn't begin doing this I hold that it will be impossible for him to get there."

As spiritual aspirants in the modern world, few of us will be able to 'leave the world' to devote ourselves exclusively to spiritual striving. That is difficult even for those who choose a monastic life-style. It is not necessary in order to make progress on our journey. What is necessary, though, is a depth of spiritual desire that forces us to struggle hard to satisfy it. Even in this early phase of our development, we have to give a great deal in order to move forward. We can only take a real step forward as we invest more of our life energy in spiritual striving.

Spiritual practice becomes the bedrock of our daily life. It will probably mean getting up very early every morning. That is not easy, if we have a family and work full-time. The depth of our desire gives us the motivation to do it. If we must struggle to reach this commitment, then by all means let us struggle hard so that we can fulfill our true destiny in this life and make that our prayer and our deep giving.

VIPERS, DEVILS, AND DEMONS

We have reached the 'narrow gate'. To journey deeper into the interior dimensions of our consciousness will require an investment of our whole being, for the way is blocked by what Teresa calls 'vipers', by conditioned tendencies in the personality that actively resist the process of purification. When they sense that their days are numbered, these tendencies fight for all they're worth. Teresa describes the situation with her familiar symbols:

> It is in this stage that the devils represent these snakes (worldly things) and the temporal pleasures of the present as though almost eternal. They bring to mind the esteem one has in the world, one's friends and relatives, one's health (when there's thought of penitential practices, for the soul that enters this dwelling place always begins wanting to practice some penance) and a thousand other obstacles.

The personal unconscious is home to a whole array of conditioned forces that work to strengthen the separateness of our ego and our sense of personal possessiveness, of 'I/me/mine'. These forces take many forms, often assuming the most attractive guises and shapes, posing as innocent pleasures and indulgences or even sometimes as the desire to help others. In other cases, they are so bold and confident as to show their real form as powerful addictions, self-destructive habits, prejudices, moral judgments of others, fears and anxieties, greed, depression, and so on. None of us are completely free of these powerful psychological forces until we master them through the battles of consciousness development.

In the spiritually-based mythology of India, these forces are the demons who are always usurping the power of the gods and wrecking havoc on earth. Demons are well known to have the power to change their form at will, from that of the most hideous, distorted creatures to beings of alluring beauty and subtle, seductive attractiveness. According to Teresa they may sometimes even appear as an 'angel of light'.

WHEREVER COMPULSIVENESS APPEARS, WE CAN FIGHT IT AND MASTER IT

Whatever shape they appear in, these conditioned tendencies share one common feature: they operate with some degree of autonomy, and always function so as to keep us unconscious. Whenever a force within our consciousness operates compulsively, we have to fight it to regain conscious control over our mind, over our desires, fears, likes and dislikes, opinions, and all manner of personal tendencies. Through unwavering dedication to spiritual practice and a continuous attempt to grow more self-aware, we gradually learn to detect the hidden compulsive power with which these forces assert themselves.

At this early stage of development, the more subtle of these forces in our mind cannot be seen. This requires the clarity and magnifying power of a mind that is held very steady in meditation. As Teresa says, the devil, the prince of deception, the power of unconscious conditioning in the mind, is so quiet and unobtrusive that, generally, many years of the most dedicated practice and inner work are necessary to develop sufficient skill and self-mastery to keep one from falling into his snares. Although the danger lessons as we progress, she says, we are never completely safe until the journey is complete.

'RECOLLECTING' THE DISPERSED ENERGY OF OUR CONSCIOUSNESS

The primary work of the second stage is to battle the unconscious forces that condition our mind, leading it down endless roads of desire, attachment, worry, fear, and so on. We are fighting to regain conscious control over our mind process and attempting to 'recollect' our psychic energy from its natural state of dispersion. It is a tough job, a battle every step of the way. In our partially conscious state, we seldom realize how distracted and chaotic our mind-based consciousness is. When we undertake meditation in earnest, though, we have to face it, and little by little, unify it, master it, and transcend it. We can do it, if our desire is deep enough, and we persevere through many battles.

RAISING OUR ENERGY TO A BATTLE-READY STATE

Teresa uses strong language to communicate the energized and combat-ready psychological state that develops at this point in the awakening process: "The attacks made by devils in a thousand ways afflict the soul more in these rooms than in the previous ones. . . The blows from the artillery strike in such a way that the soul cannot fail to hear." And when we are ready to make further progress, when we have acquired the inner strength to go deeper, we are really hit hard, for the 'devils', the powerful conditioned forces within us, "will gather all hell together to make the soul go back outside" and remain absorbed in the surface level of consciousness.

☙

We may be inclined to think that Teresa is exaggerating here. I know from my own experience that she is not. Each of us will discover the challenges of our path, whatever form it takes, as we strive to make progress. Our mind's conditioning has universal roots and is a very powerful and subtle enemy. But we are born to fight it and win. The evolutionary urge cannot be suppressed forever. We are explorers in consciousness, and this is the adventure that will claim us sooner or later.

GOD AND THE DEVIL: ARCHETYPES FOR THE PRIMAL ENERGIES OF THE PSYCHE

Teresa uses religious images and language to describe psychological realities, as of course she would, since psychology *per se* did not exist for her and knowledge of the psyche was primarily embedded in religious symbolism, mythology, and esoteric teachings. The devil is the archetypal 'shadow', the personification of unconsciousness, or rather, the power of unconsciousness as a fundamental force within the psyche. God, on the other hand, is the archetypal 'light', the transcendent, unknowable source and essence of consciousness.

The dynamic tension of these two forces underlies our whole existence, separating the psyche into a finite conscious 'mind' that has limited self-awareness, yet remains unaware of its own depth, of its true nature as unconditioned and infinite. Nearly all traditions speak of these two fundamental forces that war within the human psyche, although the concepts and symbols used may vary widely. One deep force drives us to become more and more conscious, while the other, the power of conditioning, tries to keep us unconscious.

೦3

In describing these forces, Eknath Easwaran cites an ancient Indian scripture:

> "Like a ball batted back and forth," says an ancient text called the Yogabindu Upanishad, "a human being is batted by two forces within": one, the upward drive to evolve into spiritual beings; the other, the fierce downward thrust of our past conditioning as separate, self-oriented, physical creatures.[1]

So it is—God and the devil, the archetypal forces of light and darkness, of consciousness and unconsciousness, warring in their ancient battleground, the human soul. The conditioned tendencies of the mind offer tremendous resistance to the evolutionary, spiritual urge. They are very effective in keeping our mind externalized, shallow, murky, stirred up, and weak. So we have no choice but to develop our innate capacity to fight hard to slow down our mind process, to clarify and unify it, to bring it under our conscious control.

A FUNDAMENTAL TRANSFORMATION OF CHARACTER

The devil, Teresa reminds us, works like a 'noiseless file', without being seen or heard, from within the subtle realm of the unconscious. Very often in the beginning of spiritual life, we are only aware of the unseen power of our deep conditioned patterns of thought and behavior after they have become manifest in some way that we finally realize is destructive or binding. Unconscious tendencies are hard to overcome precisely because we cannot see them well, if at all, and often enough, remain unaware of their influence.

But we are never completely at the mercy of their power. We always have some ability to explore the forces that shape our personality, our mind, even the world we perceive. When we see them, we can set out to change them, transforming ourselves in the process. It is hard work and proceeds slowly, as all of us who attempt this fundamental transformation of character know very well. Every step of real progress, though, infuses us with new energy.

Even a great saint like Teresa took many years to traverse this territory. She describes the fierce battle that raged within her as she was over and over again pulled toward, and then away from her spiritual destiny. Most of us, too, may find that our journey does not proceed as quickly as we would like. Patience, perseverance, sustained inspiration and enthusiasm: these we cannot do without.

'RECOLLECTING THE SENSES': TRAINING OUR MIND TO TURN INWARD

Teresa calls the work of the second stage 'recollecting the senses'. It is never easy to train the senses to be controlled and detached from what they are naturally attracted to, for it is our nature to seek experiences that fulfill us in one way or another. Of course, it is really our mind and our will that must be trained. We become attached and unconsciously bound to whatever experiences bring pleasure and fulfillment, and it is this attachment, not the experience of enjoyment itself, that causes bondage. Our attachments quickly become unconscious habits and take on an autonomous and compulsive quality. Then they become forces of the personal unconscious that shape our life experience, all the more powerful because they often go unrecognized.

Through relentless spiritual practice over a period of years, though, we are starting to gain some ground on these forces. Meditation, the practice of withdrawing our mind from its normal externalized pursuits to focus on a single internal object or purpose, gradually re-directs our life-energy inward and builds an inner strength to resist the 'pull' of unconscious forces on our mind.

Most of us who are living engaged lives in the world cannot follow the steep path of direct denial of our inclination to find pleasure and fulfillment in sense-based objects and experiences. We follow a slower, more moderate course of sublimating and transforming our desires and attachments, gradually integrating them into a powerful current of spiritual desire. When we work hard in meditation over many years, we will find our grasping and craving for experiences that stimulate our senses falling away little by little.

'WITHDRAWAL OF PROJECTION'

The inner work of weakening the unconscious forces that inform all our habits, likes and dislikes, opinions, cravings, desires, worries, fears, and so on, is called in depth psychology 'withdrawal of projection'. Continuously, over the course of many years, day in and day out, we keep pulling our mind's energy back from these 'grooves' in which it is accustomed to flow, and trying to 're-channel' it toward consciously chosen pursuits that strengthen our spiritual desire and build our spiritual muscles.

Meditation is the most powerful tool and strategy we have at our disposal for accomplishing this work. Whenever our mind wanders in meditation, we pull it back to our single purpose. Ever so slowly our psychic energy becomes less dispersed, more homogenized, unified, and powerful. Our capacity to be conscious, to choose consciously what we desire, feel, think, and so on, is growing.

೦೩

We can gauge our progress by the continuity and depth of our concentration in meditation, and by our calmness and even-mindedness in the ups and downs of daily life.

We learn not to expect quick results, but to keep working, keep digging, with faith in our path. That is always what has sustained me, even through some deep, dark places that seem to have no end. I have always known that nothing can hold back the swelling, inner power of long-term, deeply devoted spiritual practice. Sooner or later it has to bear fruit.

PERSEVERANCE IN SPIRITUAL PRACTICE FEEDS OUR DEEP INNER FIRE

This whole process takes time, perhaps longer than we would like, but results come, provided we persevere in spiritual practice with great faith, devotion, and enthusiastic energy. Teresa encourages us by citing her own experience:

> In order that one might understand the great good God does for a soul that willingly disposes itself for the practice of prayer, even though it is not as disposed as is necessary. I recount this also that one may understand how if the soul perseveres in prayer, in the midst of the sins, temptations, and failures of a thousand kinds that the devil places in its path, in the end, I hold as certain, the Lord will draw it forth to the harbor of salvation as—now it seems—He did for me.

Through wearisome perseverance in spiritual practice, coupled with intense longing for spiritual life and growing dissatisfaction with any lesser fulfillment, we arouse the slumbering kundalini. A deep interior fire gradually grows within us. As we continue to feed it, it gradually exerts a subtle and increasingly profound influence on our being. Some important changes are beginning to take place at levels of consciousness too deep for us to be aware of. Sometimes during a crisis or major life transition when our surface mind is sufficiently softened and opened up, we may become aware of a non-egoic power, a power that is not our own, sustaining and guiding us for a short while.

The hidden power within our being that propels our consciousness through and beyond the barrier of egocentricity, of personal identity, and reveals our true unconditioned nature, is slowly being awakened deep in the unconscious. This awakening comes to the extent that we can free ourselves from the grip of 'demons', powerful forces within the unconscious that keep our mind's energy shallow and dispersed. In the second chakra the hard work of continuous practice to bring our restless 'monkey-mind' under control is absolutely necessary. There are no shortcuts.

NON-ATTACHMENT AND GROWING CLARITY OF MIND

To the degree that our mind becomes gradually free of compulsive tendencies do we grow more calm, focused, and clear. Little by little, distractions in meditation begin to lessen, and our concentration deepens a bit. The benefits of 'withdrawal of projection' or 'non-attachment' as it is often called in the yoga tradition, are enormous. It frees us to become more truthful, more authentic, more capable of giving ourselves to others. As we learn to withdraw our unconscious projections on people, experiences, sense objects, and so on, we slowly grow more calm and clear-headed, even in very trying situations.

For many years I struggled with this idea of non-attachment. My burning question was: how can I love my children if I am not attached to them? The answer came, but only with much inner work. I had confused my attachment to them for freely given love. Attachment means, psychologically, that I am unconsciously projecting my own unfulfilled needs on someone, some thing or experience, outside myself. It is only through growing non-attachment on the inner level of our being that we can learn to see the truth in others and serve them without asking for anything in return.

Strange as it may seem at first, our heart grows soft and enlarges its capacity for love through the clarity of non-attachment. The more we can find wholeness and peace within our own consciousness, the less we relate to others, and the world in general, through the fetters of unconscious attachment. The more we are filled from within, the less will we unconsciously seek fulfillment without, and the greater will be our capacity to give unconditionally, 'no strings attached'.

THE LAW OF KARMA

In *svadhisthana* we are forced to confront our unconscious tendencies and to begin transforming the compulsive force driving our desires, needs, attachments, fears, and fantasies into energy that can be consciously utilized for spiritual development. In doing so, we are working with the law that governs the whole world of human motivation and behavior, the law of karma. The law of karma states that all human acts, including internal 'acts' of feeling and intention, have a direct and inescapable consequence that corresponds with the nature of the act.

Every inner and outer act leaves behind an impression that is retained in the unconscious. It is these impressions, according to yoga psychology, that coalesce into the patterns and tendencies that shape our awareness and our behavior. An act of grasping may increase our momentary pleasure or supply, but it begets mental conniving, separateness, and a greater tendency to grasp, while constricting the capacity for faith, equanimity, and truly fruitful work. An act of self-dedication and sincere giving may cost us in time and energy when it is performed, but we gain a greater capacity for work that will stimulate our long-term growth, while reducing our attachment to personal possessiveness.

The famous analogy Jesus used to describe the law of karma cannot be improved upon: "As you sow, so shall you reap." It very accurately describes karmic law, because our 'karma', a Sanskrit word meaning 'action', represents all the 'seeds' in the unconscious that sprout and grow into our desires, worries, attachments, and fears. Psychologically, we are nothing but a collection of these seeds, or conditioned tendencies, giving rise to the stream of consciousness we experience as everyday reality, all held together by the glue of a pervasive sense of personal identity.

When through meditation, devotion, and mindful living, we learn to practice non-compulsiveness in all actions, we are replacing karma that keeps us unconscious with karma that makes us more conscious and free. We are beginning to cultivate habits of free will and clear seeing that give us the capacity to resist the pull of strong conditioned tendencies.

It is never easy, this struggle for self-mastery, but small victories do come, and eventually, greater ones. Little by little we begin to flex our spiritual muscles and gain conscious control over desires, likes and dislikes, fears, and other compulsive tendencies. As we do, we 'recollect' more of our psychic energy and redirect it toward spiritual striving. It is like swimming upstream, going against the current of conditioning that drives our thoughts, feelings, and actions.[2] To practice swimming upstream is hard, but it builds strength and resilience and the power of perseverance.

Jung, too, acknowledged the depth of commitment to inner work that real psychological development requires:

> The way is not without danger. Everything good is costly, and the development of personality is one of the most costly of all things. It is a matter of saying yea to oneself, of taking oneself as the most serious of tasks, of being conscious of everything one does, and keeping it constantly before one's eyes in all its dubious aspects—truly a task that taxes us to the utmost.[3]

PSYCHIC FRICTION, ESPECIALLY IN RELATION TO SEXUAL ENERGY

The spiritual urge from deep within our being grows more intense and insistent as we make our way through this stage of development. The more energy we give to spiritual practice, the more we long to go deep in meditation, and, as Teresa says, the more fiercely does the inner battle rage. Tremendous psychic friction can develop between our fierce craving for the wholeness of spiritual realization and the equally ferocious energy of compulsive tendencies. I experienced this friction, and the psychic 'heat' it generated, most acutely in relationship to sexual desire.

In the early years of meditation, I became aware that sexual release had a markedly negative effect on my spiritual practice. For some days after having sex, I experienced a significant loss in my power of concentration during meditation. At first I was just annoyed, but after awhile I grew tired of this pattern. Yet, being a normal man with a healthy dose of sexual drive, I was much attached to a sexual relationship with my wife.

The tension caused by this conflict of interests grew steadily more acute over many years. I worked hard in meditation to gain some momentum, only to feel like I would lose it after having sex. I imagined myself as a hiker climbing a mountain, and every time I made a good start up the trail and gained a tiny bit of elevation, someone would pluck me off the mountain and drop me at its base, where I determinedly started the climb over again.

Eventually, the inner tension became intolerable, and I reached a breaking point. To make a long story short, the spiritual urge, the rising kundalini, finally prevailed, through much struggle and a crisis of life-transforming proportions. Interestingly enough, I did not give up sex. I wanted to, and was willing and able to, but respect for my marriage and my partner forced me to consider a surprise alternative: a creative and 'desire-less' sexual relationship that never led to sexual release on my part, but provided a means for continued intimacy.

SEXUAL ENERGY AND SPIRITUAL DEVELOPMENT

Svadhisthana is the seat of instinct and sexuality. The vital life force that animates our body and mind finds its most concentrated expression in the sexual and reproductive functions. The power of the sex drive can never be underestimated. It contains a lot of 'coiled up' energy. In *svadhisthana* we come face-to-face with sexual energy, and realize that in order to use that energy for spiritual development, all unconsciousness must be purged from it. This is a difficult task. It is not the repression of sexual desire that is required, but conscious mastery of its compulsive power, in thought as well as in deed. Mental attachment to thoughts of sexual pleasure is evidence of a strong, unconscious bond.

There is a subtle and intimate connection between sexual energy and spiritual power. They seem to draw on the same reservoir of vitality in our body and psyche. Meditation cannot go very deep as long as this energy is being released through sex. Success in meditation depends on harnessing all our body/mind energy, especially that contained in the sex drive, behind which a whole river of *prana* flows.[4]

In the second chakra, we are not yet deep enough in consciousness to get a handle on the source of sexual desire, which is kundalini. But until we are able to gain significant mastery over our sexual energy, we cannot leave the water realm of *svadhisthana*, the psychic world of conditioning and instinctual energy that gives rise to all our desires, needs, and attachments.

Eknath Easwaran has described the transformation of sexual energy as eloquently as anyone I know:

> I need to repeat this over and over, because it is so foreign to our conditioning: If you feel strong sexual desires, congratulations. If you feel haunted by sex day and night, you are a person rich in resources. It's like striking oil in your backyard; you have a little Arabia to supply you with all the power you need. Just as with everybody else, it took me many years to understand this simple truth. I too was conditioned by the media, by poetry and drama and all the literature of romance. Only when I began to see how vast were the resources

that the mastery of sex could release into my hands—to benefit everyone, to serve everyone, to lead a long, healthy, vigorous, creative life, always in security, always in joy, and never afraid of the challenges of life—only then did I begin to ask for my teacher's grace: "Make me like you!" It didn't happen naturally, and it certainly didn't come easily; it required years of valiant combat, ceaseless vigilance. It is terribly hard, almost impossible: that is its challenge. But it can be done; and when sex is transformed, the Hindu scriptures say, it is like fire transformed to light: every moment, every relationship, is suffused with joy.[5]

GROWING GRADUALLY IN STRENGTH AND DEPTH OF DEVOTION

In yoga tradition, it is said that in order for meditation practice to bear the desired fruit, our aim must be perfect. Yet, there are always countless opportunities and reasons to be pulled off course. Unconscious tendencies in our mind assert themselves over and over again, continuously testing our resolve and the depth of our desire. To the extent that we are able to overcome innumerable distracting influences that invariably tend to exteriorize our consciousness and keep it shallow and dispersed, do we then begin to make our aim steady. All personal desires are gradually integrated into a single powerful life-purpose during the course of spiritual practice in this stage and the one to follow. Our devotion grows gradually deeper and stronger.

Teresa summarizes the work of the second stage by saying that the whole aim of the spiritual aspirant must gradually become to "work and prepare himself with determination and every possible effort to bring his will into conformity with God's will." She notes that the more perfectly we practice in this way, the greater our progress will be. As we strive to purify our mind through spiritual practice with a growing inner resolve to give up our own personal life and live as the universal life, we are slowly but surely unifying our whole being.

In the second dwelling place, working with the forces of the personal unconscious, we are definitely drawing water by hand from a well, one bucketful at a time. It is long and demanding work, requiring much perseverance. By its very nature, it must be fueled by an inner 'demand' to walk this path. That is kundalini stirring, and beginning to move upward in the depth of our being.

Chapter 7

Third Realm: The Fire Sacrifice

"The whole of sadhana, the path to Self-realization, is one long struggle to unify our desires. . ."

EKNATH EASWARAN,
IN *Dialogue with Death*

THE FIRE CHAKRA

After passing through the water realm, having fought 'tooth and nail' to gain some conscious control over the forces and energies that lay just below the surface of our awareness, we reach *manipura*, the third chakra. Here kundalini enters the fire *tattva* or realm, located anatomically 'at the root of the navel', in the region of the solar plexus where the digestive fire converts food-matter into the vital energy that sustains our body and mind. A great energization of consciousness takes place in the third chakra. The arousal of kundalini takes the form of an inner fire that converts all that our senses and mind 'consume' into a powerfully focused and integrated energy. The slower and more concentrated our thought-process becomes, the more *prana* or vital energy becomes available to be directed and utilized by our will.

As the fire energy of the third chakra gains momentum, the integrative power of our consciousness grows stronger, and we develop a deeper intuition of what unity, wholeness, and peace really mean. Our mind is growing less dispersed, more stable, more homogenous, and more singular. As in the long labor of the second realm, our progress here comes gradually with much effort and dedication. But now our spiritual momentum is gaining strength.

Our desire for awakening is slowly starting to consume all other personal desires, attachments, and fears. We begin to burn with a fierce inner resolve to do whatever it takes to move forward on the difficult path to wholeness and realization of truth. That single desire gradually gathers behind it all the creative energy and inner resources that we have access to. In this chakra we are still caught in the personal karmic cycle of our mind-process. We cannot yet escape the compulsive nature of our stream of consciousness, but we are focusing our mind's energy with more and more power as we work our way through this fiery realm.

'CITY OF JEWELS'

Manipura means 'city of gems' or 'city of jewels'. In his kundalini yoga seminars, Jung called this realm the "fullness of jewels. It is the great wealth of the sun, the never-ending abundance of divine power to which man

attains through baptism." He said that it is the 'center of emotions', the source of passion and emotional energy in the psyche. It is the city of jewels because where there is passion, where there is psychic fire, where there is deep desire—there is life:

> But what is passion, what are emotions? There is the source of fire, there is the fullness of energy. A man who is not on fire is nothing: he is ridiculous, he is two-dimensional. He must be on fire even if he does make a fool of himself. A flame must burn somewhere, otherwise no light shines; there is no warmth, nothing.

If there is no inner fire burning that forces us to go forward to meet our destiny, just what are we doing with our life? Depth of desire is the expression of awakened life-energy. *Manipura* represents the power that arises when all the energy of our desire has been recollected from its normally dispersed state, in many externalized pursuits, and intensely focused on the task of awakening to That which shines in the deep center of our being, illumining the whole castle of the psyche.

Jung, however, mistakenly characterized *manipura* as a "fire of passion, of wishes, of illusion":

> As long as you are in *manipura* you are in the terrible heat of the center of the earth, as it were. There is only the fire of passion, of wishes, of illusions. It is the fire of which Buddha speaks in his sermon in Benares where he says, The whole world is in flames, your ears, your eyes, everywhere you pour out the fire of desire, and that is the fire of illusion because you desire things which are futile. Yet there is the great treasure of the released emotional energy.

Jung apparently did not understand that to reach the developmental level represented by *manipura* is far more difficult than this. It is to dig consciously into the very roots of our personal unconscious, where the powerful forces that shape our personality and mind-process reside. Here is the vortex of energy at the center of our personal being. To work in *manipura* is to harness this great abundance of psychic energy and bring it under the control of our will. The unbridled and illusory desires that Jung refers to are now integrated into a deep, all-consuming passion for awakening. The attitude and behavior he describes as characteristic of *manipura* belong rather to *muladhara*.

SOME LONG, FIERCE BATTLES ARE INEVITABLE HERE

Manipura is red in color and is a lotus of ten petals. Within it is a large triangle which points downward, indicating that the primary flow of psychic energy in this chakra is still outward into the world. Even though we are gaining real spiritual strength, having come far in integrating our personal consciousness, we haven't yet learned to 'enter within ourselves' as Teresa says. We still have a ways to go before we can step out of our shallow mind process and into the universal depths of our being. Only in the heart chakra does the prevailing energy of our being begin to move upward toward realization of the spiritual or infinite nature of existence. Here, in the fire chakra, we are still preparing for that transition.

In the focus and clarity of concentration that is attained in this chakra, we can see the energy of our consciousness flowing out into the deeper and more powerful unconscious tendencies that define our personality. In yoga terminology, these are our *samskaras*. Gradually we gain the strength and will to change these deep patterns. Some *samskaras* may eventually fall away of their own accord, but others have to be fought over a long period of time. There are setbacks at various points during these prolonged battles. There are times of frustration, confusion, doubt, and fear. But as long as we keep going, relying on the long-term transformation brought about through our deep, unwavering commitment to spiritual practice, we will pass through those times and on to new energy, strength, and inner resolve.

The deeper a *samskara*, the more thoroughly is it woven into the structure of our personality. Up till now, we could barely even see the extent to which deep, dominant, unconscious forces shape our personal life and control our destiny. It is when we are investing a lot of energy every day, morning and evening, in long hours of meditation, trying our best to keep our mind focused and vigilant, that the battle with our *samskaras* can really get fierce.

☙

For example, there is no avoiding the fight with deep fear if we want to go far in spiritual development. We have to be daring in our exploration of the unknown. We cannot remain safe if we want to make real progress. Nor can we avoid embracing the hard work of spiritual practice that seems to go on forever, day after day, year after year. And there are other powerful forces that we will encounter. Fortunately, long-term, sincere effort pays a rich dividend. We grow in inner strength and peace. We gradually resolve deep, long-standing issues in our life. That is very satisfying.

WHOLENESS DEMANDS THAT WE STAKE OUR WHOLE BEING

The animal 'vehicle' of *manipura* is the charging ram, symbol of focused energy and deep, unstoppable resolve. The whole thrust of development through the first three chakras is toward the capacity for this undivided singleness of life purpose. Kundalini, the invisible latent energy of our psyche, is aroused more and more as our single-minded devotion deepens. To become conscious in the universal depths of our being, in the transcendent core of what Jung called the collective unconscious, demands a complete investment of our life-energy. For a long time, we are working to integrate the world of the personal unconscious into our conscious will, so that we are able to meet this great demand. Jung was not unaware of the nature of real spiritual development: "The attainment of wholeness requires one to stake one's whole being. Nothing less will do; there can be no easier conditions, no substitutes, no compromises."[1] Little by little we become capable of such a total investment in life.

The fire realm is a deeper, more subtle, and more pervasive level of consciousness than the water and earth realms are. It is our personal storehouse of *prana*, the psychic energy that manifests as the power in all our desires, all passion, all will and intentionality, the very core of our personal reality. It is truly a 'city of jewels'. The Sanskrit word translated as fire is *tejas*, which more specifically means brightness, radiance, or brilliance. *Tejas* points to a level of depth within us that is the radiant energy-center of our individualized being. To become conscious in *manipura* is to live in the brilliance and heat of deep inner inspiration, tapping the core of our personal life-force.

THE FIRE SACRIFICE

At this stage of consciousness development, we perform the fire sacrifice: we build a sacrificial altar within our mind and heart, kindle a radiant fire of spiritual desire on it and begin to offer to it all our limiting egocentric tendencies, all our little personal desires, ambitions, attachments, and fears. The more we offer to the fire of awakening, the hotter it blazes. A willing spirit of sacrifice helps us immensely here, painful to our ego but liberating to our soul. It is the sacrifice of all that is small and binding and ultimately unreal in our consciousness, the sacrifice of personal conditioning to the fathomless Silence and Mystery within. We are becoming like a mother who will do whatever it takes to find her precious child who has been lost.

Lama Govinda, a European who became a Tibetan Lama, describes beautifully the 'inner fire' by which our individual consciousness is transformed:

> The fire of spiritual integration which fuses all polarities, all mutually exclusive elements arising from the separateness of individuation, this is what the Tibetan word *gTum-mo* means in the deepest sense and what makes it one of the most important subjects of meditation. It is the all-consuming

incandescent power of that overwhelming Inner Fire which since Vedic times has pervaded the religious life of India: the power of *tapas*.

Tapas, like *gTum-mo*, is what arouses man from the slumber of worldly contentment, what tears him away from the routine of mundane life. It is the warmth of spiritual emotion which, if intensified, kindles the flame of inspiration, from which is born the power of renunciation and what appears to the outsider as asceticism. But to those who are spiritually awakened or inspired, renunciation or aloofness from worldly things become a natural mode of life, because they are no more interested in the playthings of the world, whose riches appear to them as poverty and whose pleasures seem to them banal and empty.

A Buddha, who lives in the fullness of Perfect Enlightenment, does not feel that he has "renounced" anything, for there is nothing in the world that he desires, that he regards as his possession; and therefore there is nothing left that he could renounce.[2]

Tapas, literally 'heat' but often translated as 'austerity', is the psychic heat or intense internal energy build-up generated through the consolidation of desires and will into a unified force of spiritual inspiration. The fire of true inspiration, and the self-discipline that is born of it, become over time the radiance of our deeply integrated personality.

ONE STEP AT A TIME WE LEARN TO GIVE OUR WHOLE BEING

Teresa speaks of those who have endured the battles of the second stage of spiritual development and made some significant progress as "those who are beginning to be servants of love." As we slowly become able to 'serve love', we are striving to actualize the deepest spiritual potentials within our being, and working hard to root out from our consciousness all binding, egocentric tendencies. "To be a servant of love is a dignity so great that it delights me in a wonderful way to think about it," Teresa states.

Why is it, she asks in addressing the Truth that abides within herself, that when a person is determined to devote herself entirely to spiritual development, she does not quickly ascend to the "possession of perfect love?" Teresa knows that the question as stated is misleading, for the problem, she confides, lay not with God or with the laws of spiritual development. Rather, it invariably lay with our own depth of desire, and the completeness of our dedication to the path of unfolding this state of perfect love:

> O Lord of my soul and my good! When a soul is determined to love You by doing what it can to leave all and occupy itself better in this divine love, why don't You desire that it enjoy soon the ascent to the possession of perfect love? I have poorly expressed myself. I should have mentioned and complained that we ourselves do not desire this. The whole fault is ours if we don't soon reach the enjoyment of a dignity so great, for the perfect attainment of this true love of God brings with it every blessing. We are so miserly and so slow in giving ourselves entirely to God that since His Majesty does not desire that we enjoy something as precious as this without paying a high price, we do not fully prepare ourselves.
>
> I see clearly that there is nothing on earth with which one can buy so wonderful a blessing. But if we do what we can to avoid becoming attached to any earthly thing and let all our care and concern be with heavenly things, and if within a short time we

prepare ourselves completely, as some of the saints did, I believe without a doubt that in a very short time this blessing will be given to us. . . .

. . . We have our attachments since we do not strive to direct our desires to a good effect and raise them up from the earth completely; but to have many spiritual consolations along with attachments is incongruous, nor does it seem to me that the two can get along together. Since we do not succeed in giving up everything at once, this treasure as a result is not given to us all at once. May it please the Lord that drop by drop He may give it to us, even though it cost us all the trials in the world.

Indeed a great mercy does He bestow on anyone to whom He gives the grace and courage to resolve to strive for this good with every ounce of energy. For God does not deny Himself to anyone who perseveres. Little by little He will measure out the courage sufficient to attain this victory.

UNIFICATION OF DESIRE AND LIFE PURPOSE

Our task in the third dwelling place is to mold our character, our mind and heart, our desire and our will, into a deep, powerful, single-minded resolve to realize our inner divine nature. We must learn to devote our whole self to the one great purpose of awakening, of becoming conscious in the deep core of our being, and of realizing the 'wholeness' which is but dimly reflected by our personal consciousness. Only the rarest of individuals can reach this state of psychic unity and continuous single-mindedness quickly. But reach it we must, if we are to go any further on our great adventure.

The challenge of spiritual development has claimed us. We must move forward to satisfy our fierce craving for realization, for unity, for freedom from all fear and uncertainty. Little by little, as Teresa says, we find the courage and daring to respond with more determined and sustained energy. Buried in every human psyche, this challenge lay waiting for the time when it will rise into consciousness and become our guiding star. The more we take up the challenge in earnest, the greater claim does it make on us. The demand of the rising kundalini in the third chakra is for our whole being.

The energy within every desire has to be recollected and redirected inward. There is nothing repressive about this process. It is more a matter of building the power of unified desire in order to accomplish something we very much want. As the dispersed energy of our mind is gradually focused into a singular, integrated force of spiritual passion, this 'fire' of inspiration and resolve slowly acquires the power to burn through the conditioned tendencies of our senses and mind that block the way into the deeper universal substratum of our being.

"AN INTENSE INGATHERING OF ALL MENTAL FORCES TOWARD A SINGLE CENTER"

One of my favorite definitions of meditation, and one particularly appropriate to the third stage of awakening, is: "an intense ingathering of all mental forces toward a single center."[3] Only a spiritual purpose has the power to unify completely the scattered energies of our mind. Although our stream of consciousness is unconsciously generated and quite beyond our control, our human mind contains the latent capacity for singularity and unity, through devotion to a spiritual purpose. Whatever tradition we may identify with and whatever method of meditation we may practice, if we are progressing we find that our path demands a deeper and more complete commitment.

Concentration is power. The greater our ability to focus our life-energy and our mind-energy, the more it is released into consciousness from the unconscious. This concentrative power is a manifestation of the aroused kundalini. It is called the 'world-absorptive' power,[4] the potential of our individual consciousness to absorb in a single focus, an all-embracing purpose, all the disparate energies of our mind until, in the end, we transcend our mind altogether. And, of course, when we do, we transcend the world as well. World and mind are two sides of the same coin.

I remember my spiritual teacher saying that when our mind becomes steady, or able to be deeply and continuously focused without distraction, we can fight even big *samskaras* with strength and skill. Then we can transform a deeply rooted fear into courage and creative energy, or a tenacious craving of the senses into a thirst for awakening and a deep desire to increase our capacity to serve Truth. In the third chakra, we cannot completely destroy powerful *samskaras*. That requires the penetrating power of true awakening, which comes later. But when our mind becomes habitually concentrated and continuously vigilant, we can overcome most of the power and influence that deeply conditioned tendencies exert, rendering them increasingly harmless. That is real transformation.

'WITHDRAWAL OF PROJECTION' PICKS UP MOMENTUM HERE

Teresa stresses the importance of following 'the way of the Cross': "There is no doubt that if a person perseveres in this nakedness and detachment from all worldly things he will reach his goal." In other words, sooner or later we will have to give up our attachment to all experiences that tend to divert attention away from the single desire to fulfill our spiritual destiny. 'The way of the Cross' means to withdraw our life energy from personal desires, attachments, and fears, and to re-direct it to spiritual striving, to awakening to the mystery that is the true reality of our being and the whole universe.

It has little to do with the external appearance of our life, but everything to do with the singularity and depth of our spiritual purpose. We still live and act in the world, in the midst of many desires. But these desires, so present in the social and world consciousness around us, touch us less and less. Inside, a spiritual fire burns brightly. Yet we may well choose not to show that fire to those with whom we associate. Spirituality is not for show.

Attachment to fulfillment through external means, through our life in the world, wanes as the integration of our psyche gains momentum. We become increasingly convinced that our personal self is an illusion created and sustained by our mind. In meditation, as our mind grows quieter, we sense the emptiness of our personal identity and the hollowness of the world. There is nothing there once our mind is still. In this stage, a deep conviction of the dream-like nature of self and world is critical. It translates directly into a greater intensity of spiritual desire.

Teresa says bluntly:

> "Do you know what it means to be truly spiritual? It means becoming the slaves of God..... And if souls aren't determined about becoming His slaves, let them be convinced that they are not making much progress, for this whole building, as I have said, has humility as its foundation."

☙

We learn to seek, with all our strength, that which lays behind the appearance of self and world. Our whole being longs to find and serve the Light that shines within, hidden behind the movie screen of our mind. Psychologically, we are deepening the process of withdrawal of projection. Our psychic energy is being recollected and unified on a deeper level now, where the very forces that shape our personal consciousness reside. Slowly but surely, we are gaining control over those powerful forces and strengthening our inner commitment to live the 'universal life', turning to the deep unknown spiritual core of our being for guidance and support.

A GROWING SENSE OF PEACE AND EQUANIMITY

As we do, we become more peaceful inside. There is not so much that can shake our growing sense of wholeness and peace. We are gaining a precious quality: equanimity, even-mindedness in pleasure and pain, in success and failure, in praise and insult, in all the opposites of life experience. We won't perfect it here, at this stage of our development, but it is definitely growing within us. A famous line in the Bhagavad Gita says: "Yoga is perfect evenness of mind." Equanimity is the fruit of the unification of opposites within our being. It is attained to the extent that we have resolved the great conflicts that are being continuously played out deep within us. In his inspiring book *Gandhi the Man*, Eknath Easwaran states:

> "Undivided singleness of mind" is what the Gita means by yoga. It is the complete opposite of the incessant civil warfare among intellect, senses, emotions, and instincts which is our usual state of mind. Yoga is the complete re-integration of all these fragments on every level of the personality. It is the process of becoming whole.

※

SINGLENESS OF PURPOSE AND DESIRE BRINGS SUCCESS IN MEDITATION

The continuous recollection of our spiritual purpose and its all-fulfilling nature is what enables us to mold our restless, grasping minds into a steady, one-pointed state. The intuition of wholeness that comes with the growing unification of our being becomes the guiding star that leads us toward more complete surrender of our personal desires and fears, and a deeper determination to reach the 'great awakening.'

Relentless dedication to spiritual practice keeps us on track, moving forward even though we may not always see the path ahead. Sri Ramana Maharshi, the towering modern sage of south India, taught the practice of 'self-inquiry', which is the turning of the whole energy of our consciousness inward to find the Real, the source and true nature of our being. He acknowledged that this method was only for 'mature' aspirants, those with a steady mind, a deep desire for liberation, and a total lack of interest in all forms of mundane pleasure.[5]

During the course of our work in the third dwelling place, we gradually acquire these three qualifications. Then our meditation becomes deeper and more powerful. The capacity to draw the full energy of our mind inward, seeking to penetrate the silent mystery that lay under the shallow turbulent waters of our mind, is the key to realizing the true depth and unity of our being. We must be able to set aside all everyday concerns, all fantasies, all thoughts, and all sense impressions.

This is the great task of the meditator: to withdraw attention from the surface world of our mind, from the endless cycle of thoughts and sensory stimulation, and thereby discover the deeper reality of our consciousness. Sri Ramana says: "When the mind expands in the form of countless thoughts, each thought becomes weak; but as thoughts get resolved the mind becomes one-pointed and strong; for such a mind Self-inquiry will be easy." All our psychic energy must be unified in the attempt to break through the barrier of mind-based consciousness.

Remember, ego can be thought of as the 'I-maker', the deep unconscious power by which our 'I', our self or consciousness, becomes identified with our body, senses, feelings, thoughts, our whole mind process. To become conscious outside the boundary of our ego is normally quite impossible. Jung definitely said that it was. To do so, he said, would be to be swallowed up by the non-ego, the deep unconscious.

But all spiritual traditions say it can be done. The method is to withdraw the projection of psychic energy from our mind process. That is the whole point of meditation. If we are able to gain control of our mind, and hold it steady in a state of deep interior concentration, then our ego, our consciousness, has nothing to attach itself to, or to identify with. Eventually, if we go far enough, it reverts to its true nature, which is universal, infinite, eternal, whole, and always at peace.

DEVOTION

To silence our mind and truly experience the total internal 'rest' that is one of the fruits of deep concentration, we will have to draw on every ounce of desire and dedication that we can access. That is the true meaning of devotion, or *bhakti* in Sanskrit. *Bhakti* can take on several 'flavors' depending on the nature of our spiritual path. Teresa teaches a servile approach that was appropriate to her times and environment. Other teachers and traditions sometimes advise a more assertive approach that continuously remembers our true spiritual nature and dignity.

Either way, the daring "I am That," or the humble "I am nothing; Thou art all," can take us beyond ego. They are not so far apart as they seem, when we realize that the "Thou" or "That" about which we speak is our own Life, the inner reality of our very being. True devotion, of any type, demands the surrender of all egocentric tendencies, in all their subtle guises, a very great challenge for any human being.

As our devotion deepens, we begin to sense that deep within our being, beyond all the concerns of 'this world', is a reservoir of perfect peace. Our dedication to the hard work and adventure of digging until we can tap that source continuously will transform us to the core, gradually liberating us from our small personal mind-world, opening us to intimacy with the living Presence that pervades all, and finally taking us to a life of unbroken conscious union with That. It is truly a journey like no other.

THE FIERCE CHALLENGE OF REAL 'INDIVIDUATION'

Carl Jung's use of the world 'individuation' to characterize the process of consciousness development implies a progressive actualization of the full capacity of our individual being. It is a very appropriate word, for every step forward demands greater access to the energy and resources latent within the hidden depths of our being. We gain that access by facing and meeting ever new and more difficult challenges. The path of deepening integration forces us to grow, step by step, beyond our present capacity into an expanded manifestation of love, courage, dedication, and all the dynamic positive qualities we are capable of. That is the essence of individuation.

At this stage in the journey, the battle becomes rather fierce. Nothing less than a burning desire will enable us to go further, beyond the boundary of the personal unconscious. To enter the deeper spiritual levels of consciousness requires such strong sustained resolve that for a long time we wonder if we are capable of it. Always we are moving forward into unknown territory, testing, as we are able, the limits of our capacity. The inner world of our psyche, its dangers and its great potentials, are a true wilderness that each of us must explore alone. In the third chakra, we blaze a trail through the depths of the personal unconscious, battling the forces that resist the unification of all our desire and will.

We will probably feel at times that we cannot find the way, that we are caught in a maze not knowing which way to turn. Since we cannot see directly into the unconscious, we do not always know where we are. One teacher comments: "You take nothing on trust. You accept nothing but your own experience. You go forward alone, step by step, like an explorer in a virgin jungle, to see what you will find."[6] Spiritually realized beings may inspire us, awakening our own deep spiritual desire and helping to stir the kundalini power within us. They point the way down the path, but every step we take must be under our own power.

OUR ONLY ALLY IS THE DEPTH OF OUR SPIRITUAL DESIRE

We gradually become aware that we have been living in the shadow of deep unconscious forces so subtle and pervasive that we had no way to see them. When, for example, we are in hand-to-hand combat with a deep level of fear, for a long time it is bigger than we are, and we cannot see it clearly. In my own development process, only gradually am I able to grow inwardly strong and clear enough to become a worthy opponent of the deeper fears and insecurities that live unchallenged in the unconscious. The journey of consciousness exploration is a great adventure that slowly ignites our latent capacity for greatness, not in the social sense, but an authentic desire to give our whole being to the dance of life, to the challenge of developing all the potential hidden within us.

Sooner or later we realize that to tear down the wall of conditioning that the mind-process represents, we have only one ally, the depth of our desire. Nothing else can do it. It is the force of our unified spiritual desire that enables us to go beyond all personal desires, attachments, and fears. Once our spiritual passion is awakened, we begin to enjoy this challenge and this adventure of finding our way into and through the unconscious. Our whole being is gradually vitalized, invigorated, and stimulated as we make progress in meditation and in the long battle of unifying our consciousness.

UNFAILING DETERMINATION

Teresa leaves no room for doubt in advising those who have reached the third dwelling places: what is required above all is a deep, unfailing determination to reach the center of the interior castle. 'His Majesty' "must give the reward in conformity with the love we have for Him. And this love, daughters, must not be fabricated in our imaginations but proved by deeds. And don't think He needs our works; He needs the determination of our wills."

She insists that progress depends upon walking in a spirit of humility and non-attachment to personal desires and fears, with the fire of spiritual desire as our sole inspiration. We will never reach the end of the journey, she says, if, for whatever reason, we hold back from giving all of ourselves to the task at hand.

We cannot expect to reach such total commitment quickly or easily. Only when all our desires are unified does that become possible. Great perseverance in practice is necessary. Although there are no absolute rules in this respect, for most of us many hours a day of sincere effort in meditation will be necessary to gradually tame and master our mind. Through years of experimentation, I have found for myself that no less than five hours per day, divided between very early morning and evening, is necessary to make any significant progress at all. A true 'fire' of deep inner inspiration has to fuel our motivation. Until our dedication is rock solid, until our resolve leaves no room for excuses, however reasonable and unavoidable they may seem, we cannot succeed in holding our mind steady.

When meditation is deep enough to reach the roots of the personal unconscious, we see clearly the tendencies that inhibit our development, and we gradually gain the power to overcome their influence. The measure of our progress in meditation is our capacity to transform fear into courage, resentment into love, craving for pleasure into a thirst for awakening, lethargy into drive, worry into trust, self-brooding into fruitful action, and so on.[7] Every binding attachment can be turned into its opposite. We have to work long and hard to acquire this depth of integration. When we do, we are ready to reach beyond the domain of personal consciousness into the unknown depths of our being.

Chapter 8

Fourth Realm: Birth of the Spiritual Self

"In this prayer the soul is not yet grown, but is like a suckling child."

TERESA OF AVILA, REGARDING
THE FOURTH DWELLING PLACE, IN *Interior Castle*

THE GREAT LEAP TO DEEPER CONSCIOUSNESS

We now meet a critical juncture in the upward path of the kundalini. In the yoga tradition, the unfolding of consciousness from the *manipura* state to the *anahata* state, the heart chakra, is considered the most important step, and perhaps the most difficult, in the whole developmental process. For here we take our first flight beyond our mind, beyond our own private world of thoughts/sensations/perceptions. We pass beyond the personal unconscious and begin to awaken, or become conscious, in the universal substratum of our being.

This is what we have been preparing for. Through 'thick and thin' we have gradually cultivated a depth of desire and determination that will not be denied no matter what price in time, effort, and self-surrender we have to pay. We know what we want, and we know we will do whatever it takes to have it. With single-minded resolve, we 'bear down' to give birth to the spiritual Life within us.

In reaching the heart chakra, kundalini is said to pass from the 'girl' stage to that of 'womanhood'. In *manipura*, kundalini, the impersonal mind-transcending power hidden deep within our psyche, is sufficiently aroused to prepare us for a great breakthrough to a deeper and far more subtle level of consciousness. When this penetration is made, we acquire our first taste of illumination, of true spiritual awakening. This inner event, symbolized by the opening of the heart chakra, is the initial manifestation of the Self-realized or divine consciousness.

THE SUBTLE INTERMEDIARY REALM OF THE HEART CHAKRA

Anahata chakra is the abode of the 'air' realm. The Sanskrit word *vayu*, generally translated as 'air', was the Vedic 'god of wind'. He is the 'cosmic life-breath', the very life-force of the whole universe.[1] Without *vayu* there is no living being. *Vayu* is the subtle universal life-energy or *prana*, that animates all life. In the previous chakra, this energy took the form of our deep, unified spiritual desire and determination. Personified as the 'lord of wind', *Vayu* lives 'between the earth and the sky', an 'intermediary' realm between the visible and the invisible. This 'air-force' is characterized as "highly purified energy."[2]

We can conceive of the air realm as a depth of interiority that transcends our personal psyche or the lower three chakras, linking our conscious mind, normally aware of itself only as a finite personal self, with the deep universal unconscious. It is a bridge, an intermediary strata of the psyche, between our mind-based personal psyche and the unfathomable mystery of the depths of our being.

In the kundalini yoga symbolism, the heart chakra is represented by the 6-pointed star, two interlocking triangles, one with its apex downward, and one upward. Here, at the point halfway between the lowest and highest chakras, there is a balance of tendencies in our psyche: the 'awakening' or mind-transcending power dormant within the unconscious in the lower three chakras is now activated. An upward, interiorizing, and transcending energy begins to counteract the downward, externalizing, projecting tendency of our conditioned mind-process that has dominated our consciousness up till this point.

THE *HAMSA* BIRD, SYMBOL OF SPIRITUAL FREEDOM

In the yoga scriptures, the heart, not the brain, is said to be the seat of consciousness or the 'soul center'. *Anahata* chakra is the abode of the *Hamsa*, a mythical bird characterized as a wild swan. In Indian mythology and spiritual literature, the *hamsa* bird is a symbol of pure spiritual freedom, equally at home floating on the waters of life-experience and soaring in the limitless sky, beyond the reach of 'this world'. In other words, whatever the nature of our engagement in the activities of daily life, our true spiritual Self abides in perfect peace and freedom, beyond all the concerns of life and death that circulate in our mind. Heinrich Zimmer, one of the most well-known Western scholars of Indian mythology and spirituality, says that the *hamsa* symbolizes "the divine essence, which, though embodied in, and abiding with, the individual, yet remains forever free from, and unconcerned with, the events of individual life."[3]

The two syllables, *ham* and *sah*, are said to be the cosmic in-breath and out-breath, the 'divine melody' reverberating throughout all creation and "the divine life-principle revealed in the melody of the breath." The in-breath and out-breath of the human body are the visible indications of the animating force hidden within our being. The song of the *hamsa* bird, Zimmer explains, reminds us with each breath that we are divine in origin and in essence, that beyond all the myriad experiences of our personal lives, we are eternally free and pure, unbound by any conditions of bodily and psychic life.

૭૩

It symbolizes the spiritual Self, or the core spiritual nature of our individual consciousness that we just begin to make our first conscious contact with in reaching this chakra. The heart chakra represents the initial stage of spiritual awakening and is often characterized as the place of initial illumination or enlightenment. We see our first rays of spiritual light here. We have succeeded in purifying our consciousness to the point where our mind becomes, for a moment, transparent enough for these rays to break through into our awareness.

THE SUBTLE MOVEMENT OF BREATH AND MIND

In the heart chakra, the subtle intimate connection between the movement of the breath and that of the mind is alluded to, a subject thoroughly explored and developed in the yoga tradition since ancient times. As our mind becomes concentrated and steady, our breath becomes correspondingly calmer and more subtle. *Anahata* chakra represents a depth in the structure of our psyche in which the universal life-energy provides vitality to our body and mind, giving rise to the involuntary movements of both our breath and our mind-process. It is these movements that support the stream of consciousness by which we apprehend our body/mind/self and the world we live in.

To work in the heart chakra and prepare to pass beyond it is to gradually gain conscious control over the normally unconscious activity of the subtle 'life-breath-energy' in generating the rapid fluctuations of our mind-process. Now we are working at a deeper level of psychic interiority, beyond our personal identity but not yet fully submerged in the depths of the universal unconscious. Here our consciousness is becoming like 'the steady flame of a candle in a windless place', an image used since ancient times in the spiritual literature of India to represent the steadiness of deep interior concentration that comes as we penetrate beyond the surface of our mind in meditation.

The word *anahata* literally means 'unstruck' and refers to spontaneous subtle inner sounds that we may hear when our thoughts are controlled in meditation and our attention is deeply concentrated within. A whole special science of yoga is devoted to the use of this phenomenon as a method for transcending the mind in deep meditation. Absorption in these 'unstruck' sounds further calms the mind and leads to true awakening.

A MIND MADE SUBTLE THROUGH MEDITATION IS HARD TO CATCH

The subtle and elusive quality of this 'air' realm is also indicated by its animal symbol, the black antelope or 'gazelle', noted for its great 'fleetness'. Jung said in this regard:

> The gazelle . . . is exceedingly shy and elusive, and very fleet of foot—it vanishes in no time. When you come upon a herd of gazelles, you are always amazed at the way they disappear. They just fly into space with great leaps. There are antelopes in Africa that take leaps of six to ten meters—something amazing; it is as if they had wings. And they are also graceful and tender, and have exceedingly slender legs and feet. They hardly touch the ground, and the least stirring of the air is sufficient to make them fly away, like birds. So there is a birdlike quality in the gazelle. It is as light as air; it touches the earth only here and there. It is an animal of earth, but it is almost liberated from the power of gravity.

The strength, passion, and resolve of *manipura* is here transformed into the lightness, grace, and elusiveness of a mind that has been made subtle through spiritual practice. The 'web' of the world, the allurement of life as experienced through the senses and the imagination, cannot so easily catch such a mind, which has begun to taste the vastness and peace found within its own silent, mysterious depths.

THE BEGINNING OF THE END OF THE PERSONAL SELF

In the kundalini seminars, Jung partially grasped the significance of the heart chakra in the yoga system. He calls it "the center where psychical things begin," the state of development in which we first recognize and experience the psychical world, of feelings, values, convictions, ideals, and so on, as far more real and substantial than the material world. He states: "So in *anahata*, individuation begins." We are no longer completely identified with our largely unconscious mind-process. We have made contact with something greater, deeper, more universal than our personal being and life.

Jung called the transition from *manipura* to *anahata* 'the great leap'. He comments:

> So the crossing over from *manipura* to *anahata* is really very difficult. The recognition that the psyche is a self-moving thing, something genuine and not yourself, is exceedingly difficult to see and to admit. For it means that the consciousness you call yourself is at an end.

Jung's insight is important. Entry into the heart chakra marks the beginning of the end of the personal self, the elaborate but ultimately insubstantial edifice of self-identity that is created and supported by our mind, our thoughts, sensations, feelings, and perceptions. He asked the seminar attendees:

> You see in *manipura* we still don't know where we are; we are in *muladhara* just as well, at least our feet are still standing in *muladhara*; but in *anahata* they are lifted up above the surface of the earth. Now, what could literally lift one above the earth?

Someone suggested that it is the wind. Yes, Jung said, it could be the wind as spirit "but there is another thing that would make it a bit plainer." Someone else said, "the sun rises above the horizon." Jung: "Yes . . . the contact with the sun in *manipura* lifts you up off your feet into the sphere above the earth." The sun Jung refers to here is not the unconditioned 'Inner Sun' that dwells in the seventh and innermost center of the psyche, but rather the radiance of its reflection in our unified and harmonized personal consciousness. This integration and energization of our being gradually builds in intensity until, finally, we break through for a moment to the universal, transcendent depths of our consciousness.

THE BEGINNING OF 'SPIRITUAL DELIGHTS'

Teresa speaks of this realm as the place in our being where the 'natural' and the 'supernatural' are joined. We have reached the point in our journey, she says, when supernatural experiences begin. By supernatural she means that which transcends our mind-process, that which is quite beyond the scope of all our natural channels of awareness and knowledge.

She calls the awakening that occurs here a 'little spark' that in time will ignite a great inner fire with the power to consume and transfigure our entire being: "This little spark is the sign or pledge God gives to this soul that He now chooses it for great things if it will prepare itself to receive them. This spark is a great gift, much more so than I can express."

Teresa distinguishes between 'consolations', positive feelings generated through our own effort and devotion in meditation and spiritual practice, and 'spiritual delights' or states of expanded or heightened awareness that arise spontaneously and can in no way be brought about through our own effort. It is these latter than now begin. They are of a different and far more powerful nature than feelings or states of mind that we can consciously and deliberately cultivate. They are not based on subtlety of intellect, nor any kind of emotional sensitivity or refinement. They come only when we have managed to clear ourselves out of the way, to unclutter our mind, and enter into a profound depth of inner concentration.

WHERE IS MY 'HOME'?

Normally our mind is caught up in a relentless and uncontrolled barrage of sense impressions, thoughts, feelings, likes, dislikes, and so on, that fill our stream of consciousness. But now through years of meditation and dedicated living, we have gradually begun to transform this chaos into a more calm, steady, controlled, and intentional flow of attention. This slowing down and focusing of our mind gives us, among other things, a greater openness and receptivity to that spiritual depth within us which is pure Mystery, for it completely transcends our mind's capacity to 'know'.

As we learn to stop identifying with our thoughts, sensations, and perceptions, we come to see that truth or reality lays deeper than our mind. The 'thought-waves' racing through our mind are shallow and without substance, quite separate from the 'light' that illumines them. Even our personal self is intuitively experienced as a mental idea devoid of substance as well. When our thoughts begin to seem hollow and insubstantial, the 'I' behind them also begins to fade into nothingness as well. It is both frightening and liberating to sense that our mind, and our very sense of who we are, is no more substantial or real than a mirage.

To live with that feeling of emptiness would be intolerable without a strong faith and hope in the unfathomable depth of Being as our root, our true nature, our true self. Eknath Easwaran reflects: "like a traveler who grows weary or foreign lands, like an expatriate who has been away too long, you get detachment from the once-enticing sights and sounds and think more and more of going home."[4]

THE 'DESERT' EXPERIENCES

My own spiritual teacher, Baba Hari Dass, has said that 'dispassion' comes first, then illumination. That is reassuring to know. First we have to go far in de-conditioning our minds, in losing our attachment to the 'sights and sounds' of this world, that up till now have been our 'home', the abode of our consciousness, all that we know ourselves to be. To do this while yet remaining attentively engaged in the demands of daily life generally requires a long path of development. As we gradually succeed in acquiring this non-attachment and remain more attuned to the deep Silence within, we prepare for a new birth, a breakthrough into the mystery of the depths.

Before any illumination comes, we will have to persevere for perhaps a much longer time than we would like in a state of being in which the old self is slowly dying and the new is yet to come. Our personal self will not undergo any death at all without total, relentless dedication to spiritual work. It is, more than anything else, the power of our deep desire that carries us through this desert toward the 'promised land'.

To make the journey that leads to the dawning of spiritual light is a worthy challenge for any and all of us. The struggles that inevitably have to be endured here are a severe test of our mettle. Teresa comments:

> It seems to me that all the contempt and trials one can endure in life cannot be compared to these interior battles . . . that we desire to rest from the thousand trials there are in the world and that the Lord wants to prepare us for tranquility and that within ourselves lies the obstacle to such rest and tranquility cannot fail to be very painful and almost unbearable.

All struggles, she says, are finally resolved only in the last stage of spiritual development, when we have found our way home. She stresses the importance at this point of 'acts of love': "the important thing is not to think much, but to love much." Spiritual truth cannot be grasped through thought, however profound, but can be entered into through the deepest desire and dedication. By acts of love, Teresa implies "desiring with strong determination to please God in everything, in striving, insofar as possible, not to offend Him." It means devoting our whole being, day and night, to spiritual development and letting everything else go. We learn to engage in all our activities, even eating and sleeping, with awareness of our spiritual purpose foremost. We gradually become capable of fighting effectively the deeper, more powerful unconscious forces that are always doing their utmost to shape and control our being and our destiny.

We reach points in our development where we must let go of something we are tenaciously, perhaps even secretly, attached to, or undertake something we are very afraid or resistant to do, in order to make further progress. We may fight it for quite a while, but in the end, if we want to continue our journey, we have no choice but to face what we don't want to face. To do what is takes to overcome such deeply conditioned tendencies is an act of love. When we do, we grow stronger. We are no longer the same person we used to be. We have fought through some of the thick wall of fear and insecurity that lays at the heart of our personal consciousness.

ACQUIRING A 'SATTVIC' STATE OF MIND

Gradually, we gain what is known in yogic terminology as a 'sattvic' state, a calm, clear, unified, focused mental/emotional state. Yoga psychology says that the whole universe of mind and matter is composed of various combinations of three fundamental qualities that are called *gunas* in Sanskrit:

tamas guna: darkness, inertia, heaviness, unconsciousness

rajas guna: activity, passion, restlessness, drive, will

sattva guna: luminosity, sentience, harmony, calmness, balance, purity

The sattvic qualities are crucial for the attainment of single-mindedness, without which awakening does not come. By molding our mind into an all-consuming singular purpose, we establish the condition necessary for a breakthrough into deeper consciousness. By forging a unified power of desire and will that only grows stronger and more deeply determined when faced with serious obstacles that would quickly intimidate a less formidable resolve, we become steady of mind and capable of the deep concentration that leads to real illumination.

A GREAT BUILD-UP OF ENERGY IN THE UNCONSCIOUS

In meditation, the depth of our spiritual desire and purpose is gradually overcoming our mind's natural restlessness and distractibility. Our whole being wants to break through the barrier of our ego, our mind, and discover its true nature. We struggle hard to achieve a near-perfect continuity of vigilance and concentration, so stray thoughts become fewer and further between. Great perseverance and deepening commitment in practice are demanded here. Gradually even the sounds of the outer world go unnoticed for a little while, or become distant and less bothersome. Deep concentration is achieved at first for only very short durations, which can be lengthened little by little.

Jung commented that meditation, when sufficiently deep, causes a build-up of energy in the unconscious, which eventually gains enough force to break through and release unconscious content into our moment-to-moment awareness. This is how he explains enlightenment or awakening experiences:

> Now if consciousness is emptied as far as possible of its contents, they will fall into a state of unconsciousness, at least for the time being. In Zen, this displacement usually results from the energy being withdrawn from conscious contents and transferred either to the conception of "emptiness" or to the koan. As both of these must be static, the

succession of images is abolished and with it the energy which maintains the kinetics of consciousness. The energy thus saved goes over to the unconscious and reinforces its natural charge to bursting point. This increases the readiness of the unconscious contents to break through into consciousness. But since the emptying and shutting down of consciousness is no easy matter, a special training of indefinite duration is needed to set up that maximum tension which leads to the final break-through of unconscious contents.[5]

It is undoubtedly true that deep concentration is a kind of damming of the normal flow of psychic *prana* from the unconscious into the stream of our mind activity. The unconscious is the repository of psychic energy, and when the flow of that energy into thoughts, perceptions, and so on, is restrained and slowed way down, it would seem reasonable to assume that it builds up pressure, eventually causing a rupture, at least for a moment, in the great wall separating the conscious mind from the deep well of the collective or universal unconscious. Easwaran comments: "Ultimately it is in the depths of meditation that *prana* is dammed until our reservoir of vitality is full."[6]

The arousal of *kundalini* is this build-up of concentrated psychic energy, accomplished by the withdrawal of energy that is unconsciously projected into our normal mental activity. The 'coils' of universal conditioning that we all inherit force our psychic energy to flow into body/mind activity, and automatically cause us to identify with our thoughts, sensations, and perceptions. As this conditioning is 'unwound' from its 'coiled' state, *kundalini* gains sufficient momentum to bring about a momentary suspension of the mind process, very brief, but long enough to catch a glimpse of our true nature, of the infinite depth of our being and its oneness with all being.

WITHDRAWING INTO OUR INTERNAL 'TURTLE SHELL'

In Sanskrit the recollection of psychic energy from its involvement with the objects perceived by the senses is called *pratyahara*. It is sometimes explained by using the image of a turtle withdrawing into its shell, closing itself off from all outer activity. In the same way, through immense devotion and perseverance we can gradually learn to withdraw our attention completely from outer stimuli and focus all our mind's energy in an interior concentration. In the fourth stage of development we gain our first little success in this long labor of awakening in the deeper and far more real strata of our being.

Teresa also uses this image of the turtle withdrawing into its shell to illustrate the 'gentle drawing inward' that she calls the 'prayer of recollection'. These very early 'supernatural' experiences can occur at any time, not just during meditation. In fact, she stresses that we cannot of our own volition bring these about, but that they will come of their own accord when we are ready, and often when we are not engaged in any spiritual reflection at all. She says: "I for myself hold that when His Majesty grants it, He does so to persons who are already beginning to despise the things of the world. I don't say that those in the married state do so in deed, for they cannot, but in desire."

'UNIVERSALIZING' OUR CONSCIOUSNESS AND OUR LIFE-PURPOSE

Teresa is pointing out that this radical interiorization of consciousness comes only as the hold that the objects of the senses have on us is loosed, and we attach ourselves rather to the invisible, hidden, underlying Mystery that is the deeper reality of all that is. "The senses and exterior things seem to be losing their hold," she states, "because the soul is recovering what it had lost." The essential thing is that we be mindful of spiritual reality and "forget ourselves and our own profit and comfort and delight." That does not mean, of course, that we neglect our duties in the world, but that everything is done in and through the remembrance of our one all-embracing purpose.

Such deep resolve and surrender is a prerequisite for any awakening to take place. We cannot force our way into the deep unconscious, but have to make every effort to continue to prepare ourselves as thoroughly as possible and wait for the light to come. The most important quality or attitude we can cultivate, according to Teresa, is "to love God without self-interest." That means that we have to struggle hard to gain control over our impulses, our desires, attachments, likes and dislikes, as well as our fears, worries, and anxieties, so that we can give our full energy, day in and day out, to the single desire for spiritual awakening. This is our greatest 'giving' to life, to offer our personal being at the feet of the universal, to serve the universal will.

THE SPIRIT OF NON-ATTACHED WORK

For us modern seekers who remain engaged in the many responsibilities of life in the world, this means working in a spirit of non-attachment with our desires and will unified in pursuit of spiritual realization and the ultimate 'serving' which that implies. Gandhi explained non-attached work, as taught in the Bhagavad Gita, as the renunciation of the 'fruit' of action, which. . .

> in no way means indifference to the result. In regard to every action one must know the result that is expected to follow, the means thereto, and

the capacity for it. He, who being thus equipped, is without desire for the result, and is yet wholly engrossed in the due fulfillment of the task before him, is said to have renounced the fruits of his action.[7]

To go beyond the personal unconscious, we have to set aside our own preferences and desires and learn to work with non-attachment. Otherwise we remain caught in the web of unconscious, personal tendencies that inform and dictate all our actions.

Jung understood the significance of the struggle to achieve this. In commenting on the Chinese yoga text, *The Secret of the Golden Flower*, he describes non-attachment as freedom from the psyche's tendency to project its own content onto the world it experiences as outside of itself. Regarding the state of non-attachment described somewhat allegorically in the text, he states:

> This last stage, however, is reached only when life has been lived so exhaustively and with such devotion that no obligations remain unfulfilled, when no desires that cannot safely be sacrificed stand in the way of inner detachment from the world. It is futile to lie to ourselves about this. Wherever we are still attached, we are still possessed. . . . For as long as unconditional attachment through *cupiditas* exists, the veil is not lifted and the heights of a consciousness free of contents and free of illusion are not attained; nor can any trick nor any deceit bring this about.[8]

ILLUMINATION: A GLIMPSE OF THE DEPTHS

When our spirit of devotion and non-attachment is sufficiently developed, and when we have achieved a deep interior concentration in our meditation, sooner or later we will enter, at least for a very brief moment, a deeper state of consciousness than we have ever known before. No matter how brief, this experience is profoundly transformative. I suspect that there is no single description of just exactly what this initial awakening looks like. It may vary somewhat depending on the nature of the individual and the nature of the spiritual path or tradition that we follow. What is always true is that we become aware of a far deeper reality than our surface mind. Swami Ashokananda, who for many years was the guiding force for the Vedanta Society of Northern California in San Francisco, describes it as. . .

> a feeling that you have experienced a reality you had never experienced before; it has nothing to do with this accustomed reality; it is infinitely superior to it. It is more interior than exterior; yet it is not a subjective condition. When once or twice you have that feeling, your effort at meditation becomes doubled. You feel a desire to capture that experience.[9]

Teresa calls this experience the 'prayer of quiet', which, she says, is 'the beginning of all blessings'. She describes it as "the greatest peace and quiet and sweetness in the very interior part of ourselves":

> I was now thinking, while writing this, that the verse mentioned above, *Dilatasti cor meum*, says the heart was expanded. . . . To return to the verse, what I think is helpful in it for explaining this matter is the idea of expansion. It seems that since that heavenly water begins to rise from this spring I'm mentioning that is deep within us, it swells and expands our whole interior being, producing ineffable blessings; nor does the soul even

understand what is given to it there. It perceives a fragrance, let us say for now, as though there were in that interior depth a brazier giving off sweet-smelling perfumes. No light is seen, nor is the place seen where the brazier is; but the warmth and the fragrant fumes spread through the entire soul and even often enough, as I have said, the body shares in them. . . . This spiritual delight is not something that can be imagined, because however diligent our efforts we cannot acquire it. The very experience of it makes us realize that it is not of the same metal as we ourselves but fashioned from the purest gold of the divine wisdom.

Once this 'spiritual delight' comes, she says, we grow into a new depth of spiritual desire that has much less self-interest in it. Now we taste the sweetness of the 'inner fruit' and we are powerfully motivated to 'peel away' the remaining layers of conditioning that cover this fruit, which is our heart's desire. The fulfillment available to us through the pursuits of our life in the world, while we don't necessarily abandon them, seem empty and irrelevant compared with the total fulfillment possible if we can actualize our true spiritual destiny.

We gain control over many unconscious motivations that previously had a hold on us. We become capable of much greater sacrifice and discipline, so that we can undertake the journey that lay ahead, which is the steepest part of the whole climb. We begin to see the deeper patterns that have governed our being from their well-hidden fortress in the unconscious, and we have the strength to transform ourselves in whatever way is necessary in order to resolve these patterns, clear away the obstacles that stand in our way, and prepare ourselves to go deeper into the unknown.

☙

When we catch a glimpse of the true spiritual depths of our being, we touch a place of peace and joy that far surpasses anything we can imagine through normal life experience. We will want to come back to that over and over again. It is this taste of true fulfillment, true peace, that drives us forward, even if the path is steep and difficult to walk on. There is nothing in this world with which to compare it. That little awakening will lead us forward and light the way.

Chapter 9

Fifth Realm: Deconstructing the Mind-process

"This prayer is a sleep of the faculties: the faculties neither fail entirely to function nor understand how they function. The consolation, the sweetness, and the delight are incomparably greater than that experienced in the previous prayer. The water of grace rises up to the throat of this soul . . ."

TERESA OF AVILA, IN *Book of Her Life*

THE 'PURE' REALM OF THE 'THROAT' CHAKRA

The fifth chakra or 'throat' chakra, located in the spinal column at the base of the throat, is called *vishuddha*, which means 'pure'. Here our consciousness is further purified by seeing deeply, beyond the turbulence of our mind-process, into the infinite nature of our being. Shyam Sundar Goswami, author of *Laya Yoga* and a respected authority on kundalini yoga, states: "The super-purification of the embodied being occurs in this lotus through the realization of divine being."[1] The animal symbol of *vishuddha* is once again an elephant, as in *muladhara*, the base chakra, but this time it is white, the color of purity. The implication is that we have now reached the purest essence of what appeared in the first chakra as the solidity of the physical world that is perceived by our senses.

The shape of *vishuddha* is circular, and it is the abode of the 'ether' realm. The actual Sanskrit word for this *tattva* or realm is *akasha*, which is usually translated as 'ether' or sometimes as 'space'. It is the last and most subtle of the five 'elements' that correspond to the lower five chakras. *Akasha* is the substratum of all the other psychic and cosmic realms, the pure essence of matter and mind, of all phenomenality, of everything that has existence. We can think of it as the invisible 'field' on which all physical and psychical existence is based. It is everywhere and always present, in this respect much the same as our Western concept of 'space'.

We can also think of it as the fundamental, undetectable 'substance' out of which everything is made, not only matter, but mind as well.

Akasha is a deep invisible level of the 'psyche' of the whole universe, and, of course, of every individual human psyche. You may have heard of the phrase 'akashic record', a reference to the fact that this realm contains a 'library' or 'storehouse' of all the 'information' in the created universe, not only present but past and future as well. Modern physics seems to point toward something

similar when scientists talk about 'reading' events of the distant cosmic past through the energy 'signatures' these events leave behind. In the yoga tradition, this deep realm of psyche and cosmos is said to contain a kind of karmic 'memory' of all the thoughts and actions and events that take place in the universe.[2]

Moving from the fifth chakra downward, the other chakras or realms are progressively grosser manifestations of this fundamental, all-pervading 'substance' underlying all creation. This process of progressive 'externalization' culminates in the visible world that we human beings perceive, which is the 'earth' realm of the base chakra. We can perhaps think of these five realms as differing vibrational frequencies in consciousness. The earth realm, being the lowest vibration, is the most dense and physical, and the most 'unconscious'. Each higher realm, water, fire, air, and ether, represents a higher and more subtle frequency, and a greater degree of consciousness-potential.

A REALM OF PSYCHIC ESSENCES

Due to the fact that this realm completely transcends the human intellect, being far more subtle in nature than our thought process, it is very difficult to attempt to understand what it represents in the human psyche. We must remember that the chakra system, as Jung said, represents the psyche as viewed from an all-inclusive, divine perspective, one that intuitively 'sees' the whole of creation, on all levels. We are far deeper here than any cognitive capacity of the human mind can reach.

One clue, though, is that the throat area is the seat of speech, the seat of our human capacity for language and ideation. *Akasha* is the carrier of sound, or the vibrations that produce sound. In *The Serpent Power* Woodruffe discusses the ancient idea of *Sabdabrahman*, or Sound Brahman, which he calls "the immediate cause of the universe, which is sound and movement manifesting as idea and language."[3] There are similarities here to the ancient Greek concept of *Logos*. Our human capacity for ideation, thought, and perception has its roots at this deep level, where mind and matter exist in their most subtle form. So even though we cannot be aware of this realm through any cognitive process, those very capacities of our mind that we all take for granted have their origin at this universal level of depth in our being.

Regarding *vishuddha*, Jung states:

> The reality we reach there is a psychical reality; it is a world of psychical substance. . . . It is the world of abstract ideas and values, the world where the

psyche is in itself, where the psychical reality is the only reality. Or where matter is a thin skin around an enormous cosmos of psychical realities, really the illusory fringe around the real existence, which is psychical. . . . For *visuddha* means just what I said: a full recognition of the psychical essences or substances as the fundamental essences of the world, and by virtue not of speculation but of fact, namely as *experience.*

Jung clearly understood something of the nature of this chakra, although I am not certain, as is also true with other chakras, how thoroughly he grasped the level of development it represents. He does call this "the airless space, where there is no earthly chance for the ordinary individual to breathe. So it seems to be a very critical kind of adventure." He also notes that *vishuddha* is called the 'gateway of the great liberation', through which we leave "the world of error and the pairs of opposites. *Akasha* means the fullness of the archetypes; it concerns a renunciation of the world of images, a becoming-conscious of eternal things."

ENTERING INTO THE 'FULLNESS OF THE ARCHETYPES'

Jung popularized the concept of 'archetypes' as innate tendencies or dispositions of the deep unconscious to project itself into forms and images that represent or symbolize universal human experiences and meanings. He calls them 'organs of the pre-rational psyche', 'dominants of the unconscious', and 'dynamic, instinctual complexes' that form the basis for how our consciousness functions to a large degree. The world that we perceive and the experiences we have in it, he says, are 'in the nature of a symbol' reflecting that which lays hidden within the depths of our own mind.

☙

So to enter into 'the fullness of the archetypes' is to become conscious of their essence, of 'eternal things'. It means that we can no longer be involved in unconsciously projecting these universal 'essences' into images, whether those images be our everyday perceptions of the world or the inner world of our imagination, dreams, and stories. Here we have withdrawn the projection of psychic energy that creates our personal world of meaning. What is real to us now, when we reach this level, are the universal foundations of consciousness and life that are equally present in all beings.

'SEEING' THE SUBTLE MOVEMENTS OF OUR MIND

This is one way of explaining the development that occurs in this chakra. To awaken at a universal depth of consciousness beyond our image-making, idea-generating mind-process is indeed a rare kind of adventure. One thing that happens is that our mind-process itself can become the object of direct inquiry. We can begin to see how our personal reality, our whole perception of our body, our self, and our world, is generated in our mind. Jung saw that in *vishuddha* this 'world-creating' process, which occurs in every human mind, begins to be deconstructed.

In meditation, as our thinking and image-making process slows down more and more, we start to see our mind working as if in slow motion. The deeper and more continuous our concentration becomes, the slower the movements of our mind become and the more penetrating is our inner gaze. Profound concentration is like a magnifying glass, enabling us to examine in detail each little subtle movement of our mind.

Eventually, it becomes like "riding in a glass-bottom boat, gazing into the depths of the mind below."[4] We begin to see the many subtle activities of our mind that normally remain totally unconscious. When undesirable thoughts or tendencies, that are still in our mind in subtle form, begin to rise to the surface, as of course they will from time to time, we have the clarity and strength of will to 'zap' them before they gain a foothold.

GAINING MASTERY OVER OUR 'WORLD-CREATING' MIND-PROCESS

As long as we remain conscious within the boundaries of our subjective world-generating mind-process, we can never make the leap to real self-mastery. We have to get outside our mind in order to gain real control over it. True, we can in the lower charkas, with much effort, learn to dis-identify with our mind, but only to a degree. We are still subject to many unconscious forces that color our whole experience of life.

To become true masters of our own mind, it is necessary that we bring to an end what Jung called 'the interweaving of consciousness with world'. When the unconscious is no longer projected onto the experiences, objects, and people that our senses perceive, then we begin to see life as it really is, no longer 'colored' by our deep conditioning. Jung considered some movement in this direction the key therapeutic objective and an essential aspect of development in the individuation process.

In the kundalini seminars, Jung stated that an internal experience of anger or excitement, for example, is not caused by any external stimulus, but is 'a phenomenon all by itself'. When we know that and gain control over our inner world, we break the identification of our consciousness with external events. As Jung said, we pass beyond the pairs of opposites. On the inner level of our being, we cease to identify experiences as pleasurable or painful, as success or failure, as good or bad, and so on. We begin to cut the bonds of projection by which we become unconsciously identified with experiences, events, people, and objects. We gradually gain control over the ego function, *ahamkara* in Sanskrit, the 'I-maker' function by which 'I' becomes associated with whatever experience our body and mind are perceiving.

The practical benefits of this process of 'dis-identification' with the 'sights and sound' of this world are immense. We cease to unconsciously 'react' to external stimuli of any kind. When confronted with anger, for example, we can remain calm, clear, and responsive. Fear and anxiety are almost done away with. All sense of personal possessiveness, of 'mine', dissolves. We probably will not give away everything we own, but on the inner level we will cease to feel the sense of 'mine'. The idea of 'my' children, for example, is no longer real. Our motherly or fatherly love becomes universalized and loses its preponderance of self-interest. Our capacity to truly 'serve' grows by leaps and bounds.

SEEING THROUGH APPEARANCES

Yogis say that the overwhelming, almost indisputable conviction that what we experience through the senses is 'real' occurs because thoughts and sense impressions bombard our consciousness with such rapidity that they create the impression of solidity, much in the same way a rapidly whirling torch creates the impression, to the eye, of a complete circle of flame. "If objects are analysed one comes upon only subtle activity which is appearing and disappearing every moment."[5] A deeply concentrated mind, like a camera that is in super slow-motion, can actually 'see' the process of perception broken down into many subtle and discrete activities. We become completely convinced of the 'unreality' of appearances. We begin to see essence, not form. We see through appearance to the deeper reality underlying that which presents itself to our senses.

Jung was at least partially aware of the tremendous commitment necessary to accomplish this task: "A great reversal of standpoint, calling for much sacrifice, is needed before we can see the world as 'given' by the very nature of the psyche." Through a long path of dedication to spiritual practice, it is possible for us to develop the deep concentration that enables us to deconstruct our own mind-process and end the tyranny of unconscious projection and our automatic identification with the 'movie' of our projected mind-content. We see that there is no world apart from our perception of it, nor is there any self apart from our idea of it.

Eknath Easwaran describes the depth of meditation that is reached at this point:

> In deep meditation, when concentration . . . is almost complete, we do not hear the cars on the road outside or the planes overhead; all our consciousness is withdrawn from the senses in a state of intense awareness within. When we achieve this kind of concentration, we begin to discover that there is no real barrier between the world outside us and the world within the mind.[6]

As long as our awareness always functions through the agency of the senses and the thinking, perceiving mind, we remain imprisoned within our personal body-self-world 'reality'. Only when we can go deep in meditation and turn off the 'whirring' of the senses and mind, can we escape the 'magnetic attraction' that the senses exert.[7] This brings a whole new level of self-control.

HOW MEDITATION BECOMES PROGRESSIVELY DEEPER

Deep concentration is achieved through thousands of little steps forward, each one based on sincere dedication and much effort. The Sanskrit word that is usually translated as concentration is *dharana*. According to Goswami:

> Dharana is derived from 'dhri' meaning holding. Holding is a process of maintaining a particular form of consciousness without its transformation into another form. Therefore, holding is the process of concentration in which only one form of consciousness is maintained. This monoform consciousness is beyond perceptivity, intellectuality, affectivity, and volitionality.[8]

Dharana is reached when there is a continuous succession of identical 'thought-waves' in our mind. As one subsides, another of the same kind rises to take its place. For example, when our mind, during meditation, is completely focused on the thought of 'awakening' or 'transcendence' or 'God', then eventually that 'thought-wave' becomes dominant, gradually subduing all other distracting thoughts. Eventually it becomes so deep and profound that even sense impressions cease to register in our awareness. We make progress toward this immensely powerful concentration to the degree that our life purpose becomes 'single' and we keep it always in our vision, so that all our actions and thoughts are colored by that one great desire.

Gradually *dharana* becomes *dhyana*, or true meditation, when the flow of continuity of that one thought-wave or state of consciousness becomes as smooth and unbroken as oil poured from one jar to another. In *dharana* there is still an awareness of the succession of thought-waves, even though they are identical to each other. *Dhyana*, which ripens in the sixth chakra, is true quiescence of mind, like a deep clear lake with no ripple of movement on it. As we become established in it, the effort necessary to control the distracting movements of our mind can gradually be reduced until the state becomes effortless.

When *dhyana* becomes very profound, *samadhi* or absorption ensues. *Samadhi* implies complete transcendence of our mind-process. Subject and object become one. There is no longer a distinction between 'I', the 'meditator', and the 'object of meditation'. This 'non-dual' state ripens only in the seventh chakra. The progression from *dharana* to *dhyana* to *samadhi* is how the yoga tradition explains the nature of spiritual awakening.

TRUE EXPLORERS OF 'INNER' SPACE

In this fifth stage of spiritual development, we leave behind reality as we have known it up till now. The more we free our consciousness from distracting thoughts and sense impressions, the deeper we enter into the unconscious. We are truly explorers of the unknown here. This is virgin territory. As our mind slows down, so do various physiological processes, including the breathing rate. Teresa comments that at this stage, "... the soul is so separated from the body that I don't even know if it has life enough to breathe. (I was just thinking about this, and it seems to me that it doesn't—at least if it does breathe, it is unaware it is doing so)."

Normally, such a venture would carry great risk to our physiological and psychological stability and well-being. Jung pointed out many times how contact with the deep unconscious can have a 'disintegrating effect' on individual consciousness. Our long course of spiritual training, though, has provided the preparation we need for this interior journey. Still, the power of deep meditation and the kind of experiences of 'awakening' that Teresa describes can radically shift our perspective and transform our whole being.

OUR FIRST 'MEETINGS' WITH OUR TRUE 'SPOUSE'

Teresa begins using the analogy of the 'spiritual marriage' in this dwelling place to describe the nature of the interior depth that is reached. Here we have our first 'meetings' with our soul's 'Spouse', whose abode is the deepest secret center of our being. These 'meetings' represent a short period of resting in our true nature. Teresa notes that all our cognitive faculties are "asleep in this state—and truly asleep—to the things of the world and to ourselves. As a matter of fact, during the time that the union lasts the soul is left as though without its senses for it has no power to think even if it wants to."

Neither perception, intellection, will, imagination, memory, nor any other normal mind-process functions when we 'enter within ourselves' and 'wake up' in the depths of our being. Our mind-process 'sleeps' or ceases to function in any normal sense. Teresa remarks that even one experience of real transcendence has an immensely powerful effect, for it is "an uprooting of the soul of all the operations it can have while being in the body." The deeper reality of our psyche, which transcends our bodily awareness, our personal identity, and the world perceived by our mind, is directly encountered. We awaken, or become conscious, at that universal depth which is not so far from the very center, or indestructible core reality of our being.

A TASTE OF COMPLETE PEACE, WHOLENESS, AND JOY

Easwaran uses a metaphor of the Buddha, the 'farther shore', in describing what is 'seen' here: "Only after years of inward traveling, when the senses are closed to the outside world and you are miles deep in consciousness, do you catch sight of a farther shore, beyond change, beyond separateness, beyond death."[9] Teresa comments that in a thousand years of trying with our senses and our mind we could not comprehend the spiritual truth that we realize here directly in the shortest time.

At this depth of spiritual realization, we touch a little bit of 'the peace that passeth all understanding'. We are still far from being completely established in it. But when our meditation is very deep and we leave the outer world behind, we feel as if we have been "deep, deep down in a profound reality, a most wonderful reality, and the joy of it and peace of it" infuse our whole being.[10] We want nothing more than to enter fully into this complete peace and wholeness that fulfills and delights us on every level, in every cell of our being.

LIKE A SILKWORM WEAVING THE COCOON IN WHICH IT DIES

Our desire and resolve to reach the end of the journey have gained immense strength. Using another well-known analogy, Teresa compares the spiritual work that is undertaken now to that of a grown silkworm that is weaving the cocoon in which it will die:

> Let it die; let this silkworm die, as it does in completing what it was created to do.... Now let's see what this silkworm does.... When the soul is in

this prayer, truly dead to the world, a little white butterfly comes forth. Oh, greatness of God! How transformed the soul is when it comes out of this prayer ... the soul doesn't recognize itself. Look at the difference there is between any ugly worm and a little white butterfly; that's what the difference is here....

Since it has experienced such wonderful rest, all that it sees on earth displeases it, especially if God gives it this wine often. Almost each time it gains new treasures. It no longer has any esteem for the works it did while a worm, which was to weave the cocoon little by little; it now has wings. How can it be happy walking step by step when it can fly?

INTENSE DESIRE TO COMPLETE OUR JOURNEY

The taste of Wholeness that comes to us at this stage unifies our desires and will to a degree of intensity that would perhaps frighten people whose consciousness remains habitually dispersed. We become so focused on our goal that we almost 'burn' through our karma. We become very effective in battling the deeper, most powerful and subtle tendencies that try to keep us locked into our separate personal identity. We begin to observe ourselves with "acute concentration, like a fighter studying films of previous fights."[11]

We become capable of sustaining a continuous attitude and discipline of training, twenty-four hours a day, seven days a week. We know that in order to go further, all our energy must be gathered and channeled into one powerful stream. Leakage of that energy into our personal desires, attachments, and fears will prevent further progress. As Teresa says, we find no rest except in trying our best to consummate the 'union' with our 'Beloved'. All we know is that we want to complete the journey of spiritual development, fulfill our destiny, and serve Truth in whatever way it leads us.

Even at this advanced stage, there are struggles with unconscious tendencies. Some temptations we do not encounter until we have reached a great depth of psychic integration. These are for the most part, temptations of power and 'name and fame'. And, of course, it is still possible for sexual desire to temporarily overcome our discrimination. But when our devotion to the ideal of spiritual realization is very, very deep, and it must be to reach this point, we will be able to pass beyond the reach of these tendencies more easily. Constant vigilance, and willingness to fight whatever may block our path, are still necessary.

The silkworm has to die, and as Teresa reminds us, 'at a cost to ourselves'. Our old self has to die in order that we emerge as a spiritually realized being. The two cannot coexist. Our personal will and the universal will cannot both live in the same house. If we want true spirituality, we will have to give up our own will completely. Step by step we are able to do it. At this point we have 'wings', and our progress is faster than when we had to rely on the little steps we were able to take, each with considerable effort, through the first half of our journey.

Easwaran uses the example of a salmon returning to the mountain stream in which it was spawned to illustrate the total concentration of *prana* or life energy that is necessary for us to make progress in these last stages of spiritual development:

> The little creature has to fight for every foot of the way. Somehow it almost seems to gain energy as it struggles along, so that by the time it reaches the fierce currents of the mountain heights it is leaping

like a flame of prana. As I watched, there seemed to be nothing in it but pure energy, no desire except the overwhelming, overriding, exhilarating determination to reach its goal.[12]

In the yoga tradition it is said that if we attain to 'even a little truth' we become like a lion, when before we were like a lamb. Or, as Teresa's friend, famed mystic John-of-the-Cross said, like a she-bear that has lost her cubs and is intent on finding them.

HIGHER KNOWLEDGE

In the fifth chakra, our unconscious identification with the instrument of our body and mind is broken, and we realize, with uncompromising certainty, that our being is divine, or infinite and eternal, in nature. We see that time and space are deep universal conditionings of consciousness that function through our mind-process. This is not a 'knowing' of our mind, but a revelation in the depths of our being. It carries a deep certainty that our mind could never generate. Teresa describes the indelible impression that just one 'meeting' with the 'Inner Sun' leaves in our consciousness:

> ... a certitude remaining in the soul that only God can place there.... during the time of this union it neither sees, nor hears, nor understands, because the union is always short and seems to the soul even much shorter than it probably is. God so places Himself in the interior of that soul that when it returns to itself it can in no way doubt that it was in God and God was in it. This truth remains with it so firmly that even though years go by without God's granting that favor again, the soul can neither forget nor doubt that it was in God and God was in it.

This 'certitude' is called 'higher knowledge' or 'discriminative knowledge' in the yoga tradition. The word 'discriminative' refers to our new ability to separate that which is 'real', or eternal and spiritual in nature, from that which is 'unreal', or generated in and perceived by our mind. Nothing our mind can 'know' is 'real' in this sense. The 'knowledge' of our mind is always relative, never eternal in nature. To 'know' or realize eternal truths, we have to transcend the subject-object and conscious-unconscious duality of our mind-based consciousness.

As we learn to go deep in meditation, beyond the surface world of our senses and mind, and become able to do this repeatedly, the 'higher knowledge' that illumines our being transforms us completely. When we know for certain that we are not our body, we gain control over many unconscious tendencies that have their roots in our identification of ourselves as a physical being. Swami Ashokananda comments: "Only when your mind has become free from the domination of the sense world—of which the body and the outside world are important elements—will you begin to feel that the body has released you; you have become free from its domination."[13]

That doesn't mean that we disregard our body's needs. We are not ascetics who have given up worldly life altogether. We still take care of our body, but physical cravings and temptations cease to have any hold on us.

The higher knowledge of 'I am not the body' and 'I am not the thinking, perceiving mind' begins at this stage of development and deepens in the next. This deep realization and the self-control it brings, is not an end in itself, however. It is still a means by which we can reach the end of the journey of spiritual development. In the yoga tradition, the five *klesas* or universal determinants of our mind-process are not completely destroyed by the advent of higher knowledge. You may remember that these are unconsciousness, ego or projection of the 'I' or 'self' idea, attraction, aversion, and fear. They represent the deepest forces that shape our human mind, our experience, and our world.

There are three stages in their destruction: (1) thinning through a long course of spiritual practice and development, (2) their 'roasting' and consequent reduction to an unproductive state likened to that of a 'parched seed' unable to sprout, and (3) their total disappearance with the dissolution of our mind.[14] This last stage is only reached at the end of the journey, at the pinnacle of the seventh chakra. At this point in our development, we begin the 'roasting' of these deep universal forces in the 'fire' of higher knowledge.

Psychologically speaking, we learn to become conscious deep in the unconscious. The collective or universal unconscious has no boundaries in space or time. In the fifth chakra, we consciously enter this vastness, until now lost in the darkness of primal unconsciousness, and we begin to navigate our way through it. As we do so, we start to loosen the hold on our consciousness exerted by the universal forces that create our very experience of separate, personal existence. The deep unconscious fear and anxiety that permeates our human mind is beginning to give way to an infinite depth of peace and security that cannot be shaken by anything in life or death.

In the next chakra we venture further, deeper into the mysteries of our universal nature, closer and closer to the Reality underlying our being and all existence. This is the journey that truly fulfills our destiny, for we are born to become whole.

Chapter 10

The Sixth Realm: The Empyreal Heaven Within Ourselves

"We have to strip away all the barriers in order to live as part of the universal life."
THICH NHAT HAHN, IN *Miracle of Mindfulness*

THE CENTER WHERE PSYCHIC ENERGY IS CONCENTRATED

Ajna chakra is located just behind the forehead, at the point between, and perhaps just a hair above, the eyebrows. In the West, this chakra has sometimes been called the 'third eye center'. The Sanskrit word *ajna* is translated somewhat differently by various commentators, but generally means 'command' or 'dominion'. Easwaran calls *ajna* chakra the 'seat of spiritual awareness', and I remember my own teacher, Baba Hari

Dass, calling *ajna* the 'concentrator'. The energy of concentration naturally focuses at this point, and can often be accompanied by a feeling of pressure in the forehead, even in the early stages of meditation. Referring to the name *ajna*, Chaudhuri says:

> It is so called because on the opening of this center the meditator becomes the true master of his psychophysical household. He gains full control over all the efferent nerves of the body, over his muscular apparatus, his autonomic as well as his central nervous systems. He gains control over impulses and desires, over emotions, and unconscious motivations. He is liberated from the bonds of egoism and instinctual nature. He is emancipated from the fetters of narrowness of outlook in all forms.... All doubt and depression, all anguish and despair vanish like mists before the rising sun.[1]

THE INTEGRATION OF POLARITIES IN THE PSYCHE

The deep integrative, universal nature of *ajna* chakra is evidenced in the 'seed' syllable or sound that is associated with it, the 'OM' or 'AUM' that has in recent years become familiar to us in the West. It is the 'cosmic sound', the fundamental vibration of all creation. It is the sound that contains and harmonizes all sounds. Some aspirants may hear this inner sound arise spontaneously in very deep meditation. Or it can be deliberately used to help focus our mind.

Ajna chakra consists of a luminous white circle with a single lotus petal on each side, giving the impression of wings. Within the circle is a *lingam* in which Shiva appears in androgynous form. This symbolism points once again to the very deep integration that is achieved at this stage. Here all psychic polarities are transcended.

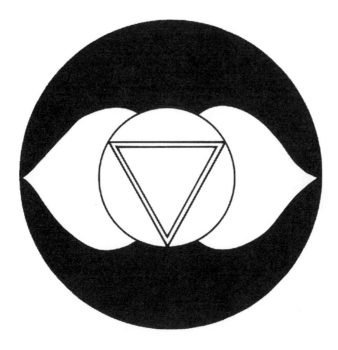

This integration is also represented in the system of kundalini yoga in another way. *Ajna* chakra is the point in the body where the three main *nadis* or energy channels meet. Drawings of the chakra system generally show these three channels going from the base chakra upward and meeting in *ajna*. Two of the currents spiral around the chakras in opposite directions as they make their ascent. These are *ida*, the carrier of female, lunar energies, and *pingala*, carrier of male, solar energies. The central channel, *sushumna*, through which kundalini travels upward, extends from *muladhara*, up through *ajna*, and on to *sahasrara*, the thousand-petaled lotus at the crown.[2]

Psychologically, *ida* and *pingala* can be thought of as the fundamental male-female, lunar-solar polarity of our psyche, and of the whole cosmos. When our psychic energy functions through these channels, and *sushumna* is closed off, as is normally the case, then we are conscious as body/mind/self, as man or woman, and unconscious of our spiritual nature. *Sushumna* represents the path of integration and unification of these energies. When kundalini travels up this single path, the polarities of our psyche are gradually integrated and transcended. When kundalini reaches *ajna* chakra, this process of integration is complete. Now we 'know' that we are neither man nor woman, nor subject to any other primal polarity or duality within our being.

THE REALM OF 'DOMINION'

When we reach this realm, we are said to be '*tattvatita*', having gone beyond the principles of earth, water, fire, air, and ether. We are no longer bound by the conditions of phenomenal existence. Through a very long and difficult course of development, we have penetrated layer after layer of psychic interiority and are now established in a universal depth of consciousness far beyond the narrow, limited, circumscribed realm of our personal identity. We have left that behind. On the inner level, we are completely transformed. Externally, though, others may not see, especially from a distance, that we are as different from our old self as day is from night. Even those we are very close to cannot really 'see' who we are at this point. But they may be witness to the 'fruit' of our development as it becomes visible in our work, our relationships, and the details of our daily life.

To become conscious at this depth is unimaginable to us in our normal state of awareness in which we are completely and unknowingly immersed in the world of 'name and form'. Teresa talks about this depth of consciousness as "another region different from this in which we live, where there is shown another light so different from earth's light" that if we were to spend our whole life trying to imagine that light, we would be unable to do so.

This is truly the realm of 'dominion'. Nothing of a phenomenal nature, nothing that is 'created', has a hold on us any longer. We are very close to, although not yet completely one with 'uncreated Spirit'. Teresa says that we are 'drawn up from the earth' and 'given dominion over every earthly thing'. The idea of dominion, or rising above the created realm of time, space, and causation, is implicit in the meaning of *ajna*.

UNIVERSAL CONSCIOUSNESS

In the yoga tradition, this state or strata of consciousness is mythologically represented as the divine realm, the heavenly abode of the gods and goddesses. Here the human being becomes god-like by virtue of the universalization of our individual consciousness. Our 'vision' becomes universal. We gain the capacity to see through 'divine' eyes, so that the whole universe becomes an open book. We experience our consciousness as universal in nature, as the consciousness of the whole universe. Teresa states, "In this vision it is revealed how all things are seen in God and how He has them all in Himself." She calls this dwelling place in our journey to wholeness the 'room of the empyreal heaven that we must have interiorly'.

Here the five lower realms are transcended and they merge into their source, which is called in Sanskrit, *mahat*. Often translated as 'universal mind' or 'cosmic consciousness', *mahat* is an all-pervading, timeless, universal depth of consciousness in which all seemingly separate life and existence has its roots. This realm lays beyond all conditioning that gives form to the formlessness of pure Being. Out of *mahat* the created universe evolves.[3] The great yogi and spiritual teacher Swami Vivekananda, perhaps the first representative of Indian spirituality to come to America and the West in the 1890s, speaks of *mahat* as the 'universal intelligence' which is individualized in every person.

Even in our normal state of consciousness, we can sometimes intuitively sense the pure, all-pervading, unconditioned self-awareness and intelligence that fills the universe. For me this most easily happens when I am out in nature and have become quiet, just observing and 'being', particularly in a place where human civilization has not left such a heavy mark. In the human world, so it seems to me, the veil of illusion is far less transparent, and we cannot gain that sense so easily.

Psychologically speaking, *ajna* chakra represents an incredible, hardly believable integration and harmonization of all psychical processes. The real power that is buried within the interior depth of our consciousness is quite dormant in our normal state of being. But as kundalini is aroused and begins to awaken, we are unifying our psyche at deeper and deeper levels. In *ajna*, our long labor of 'churning' bears rich fruit. In the myth discussed in Chapter 4, 'The Churning of the Milky Ocean', this is the time when the Goddess comes forth from the primordial sea that has been churned for so very long, granting the spiritual qualities of beauty, harmony, and abundance.

Our whole psyche becomes one homogenous, completely universal 'seeing' instrument. Easwaran states:

> Slowly, as kundalini begins to travel upward toward the fifth center, at the level of the throat, you begin to see more and more clearly. At last, after many long years of intense spiritual struggle, kundalini reaches the center between the eyebrows,

the center of Krishna-consciousness or Christ-consciousness. Then you see quite clearly. As St. Paul tells us in those wonderful lines from Corinthians, "Now we see as through a glass darkly; but then we shall see face to face."[4]

THE UPWARD 'FLIGHT OF THE SPIRIT'

Teresa says that the state of meditative absorption at this stage is so deep that the cognitive faculties of thought, sensation, perception, and so on, might as well be described as 'dead'. There is a complete loss of sensory awareness, and our breath and 'bodily energies gradually fail'. Our mind reaches a great depth of stillness.

Teresa, we know, had many unusual and very powerful experiences at this stage in her development. A variety of different kinds of 'supernatural' visions came to her. "When the soul is in this suspension, the Lord likes to show it some secrets, things about heaven, and imaginative visions." She describes raptures in which "the soul is not animating the body. Thus there is a very strong feeling that the natural bodily heat is failing it. The body gradually grows cold, although this happens with the greatest ease and delight. At this stage there is no remedy that can be used to resist." Sometimes her body would grow cold, stiff, and nearly lifeless.

Similar accounts of unusual experiences in advanced stages of meditation and spiritual development abound in the annals of mysticism worldwide. The yoga tradition covers such a wide range of spiritual paths and explorations that, of course, all kinds of radical, out-of-the-ordinary experiences have been recorded. Such occurrences are not necessarily surprising given the nature of awakening in the depths of the unconscious. "Can you imagine the effect of the sudden and massive release into awareness of what is in the unconscious? This is exactly what happens with the awakening of the kundalini."[5]

Teresa discusses how swift and powerful and irresistible was the upward 'flight of the spirit' that would sometimes overtake her. A classical 'kundalini' experience like this might be accompanied by strong physical symptoms, such as the movement of energy up the spine, or the raising of the body off the ground into the air. This happened occasionally to Teresa herself. "Sometimes suddenly a movement of the soul is felt so swift that it seems the spirit is carried off, and at a fearful speed especially in the beginning."

With some people, many different physical manifestations of the rising kundalini can take place at this stage. With others very little of this nature occurs. What determines whether or not, or to what degree, we will encounter these unusual experiences? It depends largely on our temperament and on the nature of our spiritual practice and path of development. As Teresa says, "God leads souls by many paths."

It is certain, though, that spiritual development, even at this very advanced level, does not depend on visions or experiences of any kind. They are variations in the form that the awakening process can take. The essence of development at this stage concerns two things: the depth of our concentration and inner stillness, and the degree of our non-attachment to reality as perceived by our mind. And these two are so closely connected as to be different forms of the same development of consciousness. As we attain deep stillness of mind and realize the true nature of our consciousness, all bondage to the world of appearances, of 'name and form', is dissolved.

ఆ

A PSYCHOLOGY OF THE 'GOD-IDEA'

Jung seems to have grasped something of the essence of *ajna* chakra, the center that looks like a 'winged seed', calling it 'the highest state of consciousness', albeit one that is 'almost unimaginable'. He told his 1932 audience that it was "rather bold to speak of the sixth chakra" which is "completely beyond our reach," but that "we can at least construct something theoretical about it." He considered *sahasrara* a mere philosophical concept beyond all possibility of actual attainment, but *ajna* was within the realm of what can at least be conceived of. He said, regarding this stage:

> . . .the God that has been dormant in *muladhara* is here fully awake, the only reality. . . . One could say it was the center of the *unio mystica* with the power of God, meaning that absolute reality where one is nothing but psychic reality, yet confronted with the psychic reality that one is not. And that is God.

He is saying that we become conscious at this point as the infinite depth of our whole psyche, which is to say that we become conscious of our oneness with God, who is the deeper truth and reality of our being. There is still a thin shell of separate existence. We are conscious of our oneness with God, but we are not yet dissolved into God. In the final stage, we cease to exist as a separate being any more. There is only God, or the psyche as a whole.

Jung did us a great service in presenting us with a psychology of God, or rather of the 'God-idea'. "God is the eternal psychical object. God is simply a word for the non-ego," he stated. He understood the God-idea to refer to that inconceivable totality of psychic reality, out of which our ego-self, our separate personal identity, emerges. Our little 'I' struggles to achieve an identity as separate from the whole psyche, as something real and substantial in its own right, but always and forever juxtaposed against the background of the deep unconscious, in order to maintain its own self-awareness.

The idea of God arises in our collective human experience by virtue of our intuitive experience of that vast unknowable 'Otherness', which surrounds our being on all sides, within and without. To Jung, the psychologist, that is the 'non-ego', the deep unconscious, that psychical reality from which our ego must separate itself and against which it must stand in order to be a 'self'.

"EVERY TREE, EVERY STONE, EVERY BREATH OF AIR, EVERY RAT'S TAIL—ALL THAT IS YOURSELF"

In *vishuddha*, according to Jung, the psychical fact of God or the non-ego asserts itself with undeniable force. At that stage of development, psychical reality supersedes physical reality as being the true nature of existence. There is still a 'self' that we experience, but it is now utterly transformed by its contact with the 'non-self' or the deep universal unconscious, which begins to gradually dissolve the self in its depth and 'all-ness'.

> But in the *ajna* center the psyche gets wings—here you know you are nothing but psyche. And yet there is another psyche, a counterpart to your psychical reality, the non-ego reality, the thing that is not even to be called self, and you know that you are going to disappear into it. The ego disappears completely; the psychical is no longer a content in us, but we become contents of it. . . . You are not even dreaming of doing anything other than what the force is demanding, and the force is not demanding it since you are already doing it—since you are the force. And the force returns to the origin, God.

The fact that *ajna* has no animal symbol, as do the lower five chakras, indicates, according to Jung, that at this stage "there is no psychical factor, nothing against us whose power we might feel." Our self has become the whole of the psyche. There still is a kind of 'self', but it is universal in nature. We are conscious of being one with the whole. That integration is the most we can humanly conceive of, he said. If we imagine ourselves as a fish in the great ocean, then in reaching *ajna* we are now conscious as the universal life of the ocean, not just as our own personal fish-life. In the seventh chakra, even the thin shell of our universal consciousness dissolves and we 'are' the ocean.

> Suppose somebody reached the *ajna* center, the state of complete consciousness, not only self-consciousness. That would be an exceedingly extended consciousness which includes everything —energy itself—a consciousness which knows not only "That is Thou" but more than that—every tree, every stone, every breath of air, every rat's tail—all that is yourself; there is nothing that is not yourself. In such an extended consciousness all the cakras would be simultaneously experienced, because it is the highest state of consciousness, and it would not be the highest if it did not include all the former experiences.

'IT IS NO LONGER THE SOUL THAT LIVES, BUT I (HIS MAJESTY)'

The religious language that Teresa uses expresses this same state of whole-psyche integration. One time, after having been in this 'prayer', she was wanting to write something about it when 'His Majesty' spoke the following words to her regarding the state of her individual being: "It detaches itself from everything, daughter, so as to abide more in me. It is no longer the soul that lives but I. Since it cannot comprehend what it understands, there is an understanding by not understanding."

When our mind reaches a state of profound concentration and stillness, and the normal processes of thought, perception, and so on, are not functioning, when body and world and self are no longer 'in' our consciousness, we cannot help but 'see' that we are the whole, the Light that shines in and through all that is. Teresa explains that "...the faculties and the whole interior stop in such a way that the soul sees clearly that another greater Lord than itself governs that castle. And this brings it deep devotion and humility." She says that our being is 'joined to God', and the indelible impression that this 'union' leaves convinces us deeply that it is true.

We cannot grasp the nature of this deep integration of our being intellectually. Even depth psychology cannot understand it. The study of dreams, myths, archetypes, and so on, can point to possibilities, but this is an indirect method of inquiry that cannot directly illumine the deep unconscious. How can our personal intellect understand that which is universal, spiritual, and transcendent in nature? How can an ant understand human civilization? What depth psychology can do, though, is provide us with a viable language for even talking about the psyche as a whole, and the path of integration and unification that leads to an expansion and development of all our consciousness-potentials.

'WOUNDED WITH LOVE' BY A SPARK OF THE 'INFINITE FIRE'

This stage, Teresa says, confers great strength to follow the dictates of 'God's will' or what psychologically we can call the 'universal will', that deep inner wisdom and will that comes when we tear down the edifice of personal identity and desire that has dominated human consciousness for eons. That 'universal will' now begins to guide our every action. "From here on the soul desires nothing for itself; it wants its actions to be in complete conformity with His glory and His will." We do all that is asked of us, and what formerly was very difficult now becomes easy, because our resistance is gone. We may end up doing very different things than we have ever imagined. Because the desires and fears of the personal self have been left behind, we reach now into a deep well of strength, far greater than anything our personal consciousness can generate.

Teresa speaks of this dwelling place as one in which we are 'wounded' with love for our 'Spouse', the deep interior One who is our true life and being. She compares this 'wound of love' to a spark of fire that has leapt forth from the 'Infinite Fire' in the center of our being and struck our consciousness so that we feel that Fire. But our being is not "set on fire" and consumed quite yet because "just as the fire is about to start, the spark goes out and the soul is left with the desire to suffer again that loving pain the spark causes."

She makes many references to the keen suffering that she experienced at this point in her journey and that others may, or may not, experience, saying that it is truly 'no less than death'. It is not easy, from our vantage point, to understand just what this deep suffering consisted of. For Teresa, it was at times physical in nature as the experiences of rapture and absorption that she underwent were sometimes quite extreme and very hard on her body. But it was also a deep emotional suffering, a 'dying' onto herself, accompanied by a very great longing for the state of complete and continuous union in which there is no 'self' left to suffer.

☙

She tells us clearly how every fault, every shortcoming, every 'speck of dust' in our character is now 'seen', especially as we are very near the pure radiance of the 'Inner Sun'. In this stage, she says, "...deep humility is impressed upon the soul." This deep suffering comes in order that we may enter the seventh dwelling place. It is a suffering that none of us, having come this far, would want to resist.

THE 'PLEDGE OF BETROTHAL'

"As a result of these wonderful favors the soul is left so full of longings to enjoy completely the One who grants them that it lives in a great though delightful torment." I suspect that all spiritual aspirants, regardless of the nature of our path and the way it unfolds, must feel something of both very deep joy and very deep longing at this stage. Returning to her use of the courtship and marriage analogy to illustrate these last stages of spiritual development, Teresa says:

> Now the soul is fully determined to take no other spouse. But the Spouse does not look at the soul's great desires that the betrothal take place. For He still wants it to desire this more, and He wants the betrothal to take place at a cost; it is the greatest of blessings. . . . for the soul to endure such delay it needs to have that token or pledge of betrothal that it now has.

The sixth stage is our 'engagement' period in which we must wait for the time of final consummation of the marriage or union to take place. Even though we are awake and conscious at the universal level, at least during meditation, there is still one barrier left to tear down if we are to realize complete wholeness. A persistent layer of universal mind-conditioning is still present, creating a thin 'veil' of separateness between our 'self' and the core reality of our being, that which truly is our Life and our Being. Our anticipation of, and desire for, the final 'union' is very great.

Our desire is not always satisfied as quickly or easily as we would like, though, for we must still realize complete 'desirelessness', including non-attachment to any unusual psychic capacities and powers that either come unsought or can be deliberately cultivated at this stage of practice. We have to 'abandon all supports'. "This is terribly difficult advice, because it means not to hold on to anything on earth—any material thing, any person, any source of satisfaction. If we are trying to hold on to anything external, we cannot hold on wholly to the Self."[6]

THE FINAL 'KNOT' OF CONDITIONING THAT WE MUST UNDO

The Sanskrit word *siddhi*, which literally means 'perfection', generally refers to supernormal powers over matter and mind. These can be cultivated through concentration and austerity. They come unsought to some aspirants, but, generally they must be cultivated, and most aspirants have neither any need nor desire to do so. In the *Yoga Sutras* various incredible powers of the body, senses, and mind are enumerated and explained, after which it is stated that these powers are "acquisitions in a normal fluctuating state of the mind" but "impediments to samadhi."[7] They are worldly attainments, albeit very unusual ones, but they cannot lead to the cessation of our mind-process and the end of all separateness. Swami Vivekananda says in this regard:

> Different powers will come to the Yogi, and, if he yields to the temptation of any one of these, the

road to his further progress will be barred.... But if he is strong enough to reject even these miraculous powers, he will attain to the goal of Yoga, the complete suppression of the waves in the ocean of the mind.[8]

In the yoga tradition, there are said to be three 'knots' of deep conditioning that have to be undone during the course of spiritual development. The first knot is in the base chakra and concerns our attachment to the world of 'name and form', to the world of appearances and the objects that our senses are attracted to. The second knot is in the heart chakra and concerns our identification as a 'self'. The final knot that we must untie in our quest for wholeness is encountered only in this sixth stage and requires our complete non-attachment, even to universal knowledge and power.

A POINT OF MAXIMUM CONCENTRATION AND ILLUMINING POWER

Teresa comments that "whoever stands upon a height sees many things." An expansion of our mind's 'seeing' capacity comes naturally through depth of concentration. When the flow of our attention is as smooth as the flow of oil from one jar to another, and there are no breaks in it caused by distracting thoughts or sense impressions, we have reached as pure and powerful a state of mind as can be humanly achieved. In this state our mind reflects, or takes the form of the infinite. But it is still a mind-state.

> Dhyana is that state of consciousness in which the body becomes completely motionless like a mountain; the senses of smell, taste, sight, touch and sound become inoperative, and consequently, the outer world is no longer the content of

consciousness; consciousness remains unaffected by intellective functions and thoughts; such consciousness, thus being empty, coils to a point in which all its power is in full concentration.[9]

This 'point' of maximum concentration and power is called *'bindu'* in Sanskrit. When the energy of our consciousness is compressed into a single point and held very steady, our mind acquires a great power of illumination and penetration. Time dissolves, and past and future come and 'stand' in the present. This state can be highly developed, to the point, yogis say, where cognitive capacity is virtually unlimited. Knowledge of present, past, and future comes simultaneously, and all that is to be known about something is known at once.[10]

Such powers as these, however, although they represent the highest capacities our mind can realize, are not requirements for liberation. Most of us will not pursue their attainment. Any attachment, even to omniscience, will hold us back and block our entry into the final stage in the full integration of our being.

CROSSING THE GREAT CHASM IN OUR PSYCHE BETWEEN SEPARATENESS AND UNITY

Eventually true 'union' comes. Our mind-process is completely transcended, even its most universal manifestation, and with it all traces of separateness end. In *ajna* chakra as our mind grows deeper in stillness and purity, it reflects more and more of the all-radiance of *sahasrara*. We have come very far in crossing the psychic 'chasm' between our personal self and the Whole, but there is still a final leap that must be made to complete the journey. It requires a maximum effort to dissolve all subtle attachments that still linger in our consciousness. We must 'die' unto ourselves completely, in order to 'be' the Whole, the Life of our life and of the whole universe.

The foremost requirement for crossing that last threshold is the totality and utter depth of our desire and resolve to reach the 'promised land' of wholeness, peace, and freedom. Twenty-four hours a day we live with that one purpose in mind. Our psychic energy must be fully unified. The tightly wound 'coils' of conditioning that generate our mind-process have to be fully and permanently 'uncoiled'. We have to gain continuous control of our mind-process, so that lapses in concentration cease to occur.

Of course, we continue to fulfill our duties in life, and all subtle self-interest is left behind, in our relationships, in our work, in all our activities. As Teresa says, "The soul desires to be completely occupied in love and does not want to be taken up with anything else." The world of appearances that is cognized by our senses and our mind no longer has any hold on us at all. We function in it, but are not touched by it. Teresa calls this world a 'complete lie and falsehood'. To our thinking, perceiving mind, of course, it seems so very 'real'. But now we are conscious at a far more fundamental level of existence, and we see right through the whole realm of 'name and form' to the deeper Truth underlying it.

We cut all subtle bonds of attachment that may still remain. When we become established in extreme non-attachment and extreme desire for liberation or 'union', we leave all doubt, all fear, and all sorrow behind. Our old 'self' is dead. We are ready for the culmination of our long journey.

Chapter 11

The Seventh Realm: The 'Peace that Passeth All Understanding'

"In the end, people must always live with fear until You give them true peace and bring them there where that peace will be unending."

TERESA OF AVILA, IN *Interior Castle*

THE 'FULL MOON' OF THE 'THOUSAND-PETALED' LOTUS

*K*undalini now reaches its final destination in the 'thousand-petaled' lotus. The name *sahasrara* means 'thousand-petaled'. This chakra is also called *sunya*, which means 'empty' or 'void', and *niralambapuri*, which means 'dwelling place without support'.[1] The form of the chakra is that of a circle, like a full moon, encircled with an 'umbrella' of one thousand lotus petals of all the colors of the rainbow. Its location is the crown of the head, or some say, just slightly above the crown. Easwaran hints at one reason why the explosion of a thousand petals occurs here: "When, after many years of sincere effort in meditation, kundalini finally reaches the crown of the head, the billions of cells in the brain all burst into integrated activity."[2]

We have reached the ultimate harmony. The full moon in *sahasrara* symbolizes the perfect integration, harmonization, and illumination of our whole being. The nectar of supreme peace flows uninterruptedly. In the yoga tradition, this is liberation. We are *jivan mukta*, 'free while living'.

Some yoga texts and commentators speak of a number of minor chakras that lay between *ajna* and *sahasrara*, or are included as part of *sahasrara*. These refer to various stages and states in the final and complete awakening of kundalini. One of these, for example, is called *soma* chakra.[3] *Soma* means 'nectar' and 'the moon'. It is also called *amrita* chakra, which means nectar as well. Due to the deep unification taking place in the depths of our being, 'a constant and profuse stream of nectar-like essence' flows into our consciousness, especially during meditation. We abide in true spiritual peace, joy, and harmony.

BURSTING THE BONDS OF CONDITIONING AND REALIZING OUR PURE, INFINITE NATURE

In moving from *ajna* to *sahasrara* kundalini at last bursts the bonds of all conditioning, breaking through the final 'veil' of 'universal mind'. Unconditioned consciousness is free of all fluctuations, free of all mind-process. Our mind just disappears when we realize total stillness. We are completely conscious. Mind-conditioning implies partial

unconsciousness, a limitation of consciousness in which a split between subject and object appears, the endless whirring of our mind-process is activated, and the world of 'name and form' is projected outward. Unconditioned or complete consciousness is pure Spirit.

Kundalini is the power and potential deep within us to undo all our conditioning as 'created' beings, to transcend the world of matter and mind, and to realize our true identity as Spirit, as Infinite Life. The awakening of kundalini is a reversal of the 'world-creating' process of our mind. As the deep unconscious forces in our psyche that generate this process are resolved and eventually destroyed, we become conscious as that which we truly are and the world truly is, God, or 'Uncreated Spirit', the very Life and Light of all beings. Our evolutionary destiny is fulfilled. The conscious-unconscious polarity of our being is resolved, and we are whole, unified, as Easwaran says, 'from surface to seabed'.

IMPOSSIBLE!! COMPLETE CONSCIOUSNESS??

Jung could not accept this possibility. Regarding the seventh chakra, he said:

> To speak about the lotus of the thousand petals above, the *sahasrara* center, is quite superfluous because that is merely a philosophical concept with no substance to us whatever; it is beyond any possible experience. In *ajna* there is still the experience of the self that is apparently different from the object, God. But in *sahasrara* one understands that it is not different, and so the next conclusion would be that there is no object, no God, nothing but Brahman. There is no experience because it is one, it is without a second. It is dormant, it is not, and therefore it is *nirvana*. This is an entirely philosophical concept, a mere logical conclusion from the premises before. It is without practical value for us.

For Jung, our ego or mind 'is' consciousness. To transcend it is to go completely 'unconscious'. How can there be a 'conscious' experience if the mind and the self are dissolved? Who is left to experience anything? Yes, there is no one left, we might reply, there is only Spirit, which is Consciousness Itself. To those who see through the eyes of their mind, though, there is still the 'appearance' of one who eats, talks, and acts. The possibility that a human being can be 'completely conscious' without any 'other' to be conscious 'of' is indeed a supreme mystery. That is why our path demands deep 'faith'. Our reasoning mind cannot fathom Unity.

ALL FEAR VANISHES, AND OUR PEACE KNOWS NO LIMITS

Of course, there is and can be no 'objective' proof of the claim of God-realization. Subjectively, though, there is proof of 'union'. All fear vanishes. As long as there is any separateness or duality in our psyche, fear will not completely leave our consciousness. But when we become established in complete unity or non-duality, no fear remains. It disappears with our mind-process. Fear can come only when our mind fluctuates. When it is still, there is only the infinitely deep well of true peace. Teresa states that "in the end, people must always live with fear until You give them true peace and bring them there where that peace will be unending."

Death is no longer a mystery, nor does it give rise to any fear. Teresa tells us that we will have no more fear of death than of a 'gentle rapture'. The ending of consciousness and life-energy in our body is not such a big deal when our consciousness and life is no longer localized in our body. For a spiritually realized being, "body and mind are only a kind of jacket. His consciousness is no more ruptured by death than ours is when we take off a jacket at night."[4]

We have already learned, in the depth of our meditation, to completely withdraw all psychic energy from the instrument of our body and mind, into the spiritual core of our being, where there is no birth or death. If we are fully established in that depth, we will remain conscious right through the doorway of death. Easwaran comments that a liberated being...

> can travel with a dying person across the threshold of life and death, from the far side of which no separate individual can return in this same life. If

the dying person has a deep bond of love for you, that love is a channel through which you can communicate your personal realization: that death is not the end of the story but only a door, a gate, a bridge, through which we pass to rest a while before we come back to pick up our evolution where we left off. To somebody who understands this, death loses its terrors.[5]

UNION WITH GOD, OUR SOURCE, OUR LIFE, OUR ALL

In the seventh dwelling place, the 'spiritual marriage' between our purified individual consciousness and the 'Inner Sun' who gives it life and being, is finally consummated. Our 'soul' or psyche transcends its inherent duality and realizes wholeness. The limitations of our mind disappear altogether, and our consciousness reverts to its true nature, beyond conception, beyond imagination, beyond fear and sorrow, beyond all that is finite.

Like 'seers' in many traditions, Teresa expresses this unified state of 'complete consciousness' as the union of the soul with God. Through the imagery of the interior castle, she helps us to understand that God, the source of all 'light' or consciousness and life, dwells within our most interior depth. God is truly our life and our being. By undertaking a journey into our own unknown interior realms, we can 'peel away' the coverings that hide our true Life from us. Upon reaching 'His Majesty's' home in the deepest secret chamber of our being, all the coverings are stripped away, and we abide in and as pure Spirit, for that is our true nature. We enjoy perfect peace.

In order to enter permanently into the seventh mansion, Teresa reminds us that we must realize complete non-attachment to everything in the physical and psychical universes. 'This little bird', as she sometimes calls our personal consciousness, must die before it can be reborn as one with 'uncreated Spirit'. The tiny stream of our personal consciousness cannot flow into the great expanse of the ocean of being, until we have been very thorough in removing from ourselves all subtle tendencies toward separate existence. It is never easy to let go of all that we cling to and willingly release our whole being into the great Mystery.

The whole message of *Interior Castle* is that in the deepest core of our being, we are one with God or Spirit. The center of our being, Teresa says, is a 'room' where only 'His Majesty' dwells. Of course as long as there is a body that acts in the world, there is the appearance of duality, but that in no way negates that in the interior of our being we always remain conscious as the Whole, indivisible and uncreated in nature. Teresa states that "the essential part of her soul never moved from that room" in which Spirit dwells, despite many outer trials and business affairs that she had to attend to.

"WHEN A LITTLE STREAM ENTERS THE SEA, THERE IS NO MEANS OF SEPARATING THE TWO"

Teresa says that there is the 'greatest difference' between the 'union' that takes place here and that which occurs in the previous dwelling place. It is the same, she says, as the difference between two people who are 'betrothed' and two who have become united, never again to be separated.

> What God communicates here to the soul in an instant is a secret so great and a favor so sublime—and the delight the soul experiences so

extreme—that I don't know what to compare it to. I can say only that the Lord wishes to reveal for that moment, in a more sublime manner than through any spiritual vision or taste, the glory of heaven. One can say no more—insofar as can be understood—than that the soul, I mean the spirit, is made one with God. For since His Majesty is also spirit.

In this marriage or union, "the soul always remains with its God in that center." It is "like what we have when a little stream enters the sea, there is no means of separating the two. Or like the bright light entering a room through two different windows; although the streams of light are separate when entering the room, they become one." Teresa is here using classic images of non-duality. She leaves no doubt that the spiritual marriage is not a union of two who remain united but separate by virtue of possessing innately different natures. No, we become consciously one with Spirit in the seventh dwelling place, because Spirit or infinite being, is our very nature. All mind-conditioning has been removed, and we are conscious in the pure spiritual center of our being.

Of course, the One who dwells in that deepest core of our being has always been present there, being the source of all light or consciousness everywhere in the castle and outside as well. In that center, there is no darkness, for the nature of God or Spirit is pure light, pure consciousness in which no unconsciousness exists. "Everything corporeal in the soul" is "taken away," and the soul is "left in pure spirit. Thus the soul could be joined in this heavenly union with the uncreated Spirit." Teresa clearly paints a picture here of a state of 'oneness' that is beyond all opposites, beyond all separateness, and beyond all boundaries and divisions.

☙

'ALMOST TOO GREAT A REVELATION TO ABSORB'

Eknath Easwaran marvels at this 'Land of All Light', this complete consciousness, that is the miracle hidden deep in the center of our being:

> . . .our real personality is all light, all love, always shining. As Saint Teresa of Avila testifies, it is day without night, a world of perpetual light. Even the sun and stars borrow light from the light of consciousness. . .
>
> It is almost too great a revelation to absorb. Yet when I look at the sun now, I remember the penetrating words my spiritual teacher spoke to me many years ago: "One day that sun will burn out, but *you* will never die.[6]

What a tremendous leap of faith is required to believe in this possibility, to the point where we will pursue it year after year, decade after decade until finally, faith becomes reality. Teresa tells us that this indestructible, self-luminous core of our being is "something so difficult to explain, and even believe in, that I think, Sisters, I'll not give you the temptation to disbelieve what I say, for I do not know how to explain this center."

If we cannot yet see the unimaginable beauty of this castle that is our being, Teresa says, it is not because that beauty is lacking in us, for it exists in equal measure in every person. The 'shining sun' that is hidden in the center of our being never fades. Its beauty and brilliance are always present. It is just that our rapidly fluctuating mind-process, which is unconsciously generated, disturbs and clouds up our consciousness to such a degree that, even though some light still comes through, we lose all awareness of the source of that light. The cloudy, agitated waters of our mind effectively block most of the light. We are conscious, but cut off from the source of consciousness within us. So we undertake the journey of spiritual development to re-establish our oneness with that source.

A 'CLOUD OF MAGNIFICENT SPLENDOUR'

In describing how she entered the final dwelling place, Teresa says: "First there comes an enkindling in the spirit in the manner of a cloud of magnificent splendour." She explains that in her own case, she had a vision of Christ in which He "told her that now it was time that she consider as her own what belonged to Him and that He would take care of what was hers, and He spoke other words destined more to be heard than to be mentioned." Teresa was of a temperament that was given to 'visions'. Many of us are not so inclined, and she acknowledges that with others this 'favor' will come in a different form.

The 'cloud' that Teresa describes has a parallel in the yoga tradition. When we have reached the state of *dhyana* or deep, smooth, unbroken interior concentration and have forsaken all attachments, including supra-ordinary knowledge or powers, that would keep alive our separate identity, then we reach the state called *dharma-megha* or 'virtue-pouring cloud'. *Dharma* is a word with several meanings, but here it signifies the fullness of virtue that 'rains' down on our being.

In this state, we become completely 'saturated' with the deep joy and peace of pure, unconditioned, infinite consciousness. "As a cloud pours rain so this Samadhi pours the highest virtue" and "success in then attained without effort."[7] All separateness disappears. When no desires or attachments of any kind are left, our mind becomes pure and reverts to its true nature. Only then does all fear and all sorrow depart for good. Truth becomes real to us, the only reality. 'Peace and calmness, and perfect purity' become our own nature, after giving up the 'vanity of powers'.[8]

THE DISSOLUTION OF OUR MIND-PROCESS

It is the supreme renunciation of all 'knowables' that leads to the final cessation of all the fluctuations of our mind. Everything that can be 'known' or apprehended by our mind is 'appearance' only. As we progress through the fourth through sixth stages we come to realize that our mind projects 'name and form' onto everything. This is its 'world-creating' function. Consciousness divides into self and world. When our mind becomes increasingly steady and still we see that behind it all is Unity. There is only God, 'One-without-a-second'.

Sooner or later, during deep meditation, we enter into that Unity and our separate self disappears. But when we come out of that meditation, it is still there, and our mind-process starts up again. Over and over again, we have to enter into that unimaginable state in which our mind-process is 'arrested', completely devoid of fluctuations. Eventually, that 'arrested' state becomes permanent. It is then that our mind and our 'self' finally die. This is liberation, which only comes when the 'arrested' state of mind or complete inner stillness, remains unbroken and the last vestige of 'I-sense', which is the root of our mind, has completely dissolved.

The death of our mind and the death of our 'I-sense' are one and the same. There can be no thought or sense perception without reference to the subject 'I'. That is why our spiritual path is always one of deeper non-attachment, of 'giving up everything', of withdrawing the projection of psychic energy by which 'I' becomes identified with all that our body-mind experiences. That, of course, does not mean sitting in a cave all day. It means an inner renunciation of all sense of separate self-identity and self-will, all sense of 'I' as something that exists and acts, apart from the Whole. It means total, unwavering dedication to dismantling and dissolving our self-identity in the deep Mystery that is our true identity. It means dying to self and world so that we may live as spiritual Being.

WHEN WE HAVE REALIZED THE 'STATE OF YOGA'

When we are established in Unity, the primal separation of our being into conscious and unconscious is finally gone. We are made whole, and that wholeness is a mystery that the human mind, based as it is on duality, cannot fathom. The last unconscious impressions that are still left in our mind in this final dwelling place are those of the 'arrested' state itself. As we become permanently established in stillness, these impressions, now all that's left of what we call the unconscious, no longer serve any purpose and disappear for lack of use. Then our mind is pure and remains always completely conscious and quiescent. The karmic 'wheel of fluctuations and impressions' that is, or was, our mind-process is put to rest for good.

This is *nirvana*, which means the state of having been 'blown out' or extinguished. When our mind is extinguished, all we see is God or Consciousness everywhere because 'seer' and 'seen' have realized their indivisibility, and there is nothing else. Inner-outer, past-future, birth-death, pleasure-pain, all opposites die with our mind. There is only the Real, the One-without-a-second. There is no 'other', no phenomena, no coming and going, no birth, no death, no bondage, no liberation, no 'I', no 'you', only Truth abiding in its own nature. We have realized the 'state of yoga': *Yoga cittavritti nirodha*. This is the famous definition of yoga given in the second verse of the Yoga Sutras: 'Yoga is the cessation of the fluctuations of the mind'.

A MIND-PROCESS CAN BE REACTIVATED WHEN NEEDED

When we have become established in unity or non-duality, our mind is 'like a hailstone fallen in the ocean', dissolved in the ocean of infinite consciousness. Of what shall we be afraid? There is nothing outside our own Being. The appearance of a separate self, and a separate world, is gone.

> The perception of plurality ceases, meaning, no more do we see the objects as distinctly separate, but in that new Light-of-wisdom, all of them coalesce to be the One, shining in their new garment of Beauty-Peace-Truth. The names and forms are there, but in and through them all, we come to see the Truth, the Reality, everywhere.[9]

The dissolution of our mind does not mean that we are incapable of functioning in the world. When there is a need, a mind-process is activated, but it is not 'ours'. We do not identify with it at all. There is no compulsion in it, and no karma is generated. "Once we finally enter the unitive state, our passport is good in both worlds. We can learn to function freely in the world of duality, yet we never forget who we are and where we really live."[10] We gain the ability to use a mind-process in order to do whatever we are led to do, but it comes and goes as we choose, and we are not bound by it.

Having permanently stilled the mind, it can never again start up as an unconsciously-generated, dualistic process. No impressions are generated when it is used as an instrument for acting in the world. It is a tool, a very clear, effective one, that is now provided for our use by nature, just as a body is provided by nature as well. But they remain only appearances in a world of names and forms that, in and of themselves, have no more reality than a shadow does, in and of itself.

THE 'JACKET' OF PERSONAL IDENTITY

To others it may appear that the spiritually illumined being acts with self-interest just as everyone does. In a way, it is true. On the outer level, it is impossible to act in this world without a kind of 'ego'. We can still 'put on' an appearance of personal identity, but it is 'only an outer covering, like a coat or a mask' which we can 'assume or lay aside' as we choose. Our thoughts, words, and actions "are said to be like 'burnt seeds'—that is to say, they are no longer fertile; they cannot bring forth any more samskaras, they cannot create any new addiction or bondage."[11] Never for an instant do we forget that the world is an appearance, and that Truth shines as the 'substance' and deeper reality of that which appears as 'world'.

Teresa alludes to the complete continuity of spiritual realization, within her consciousness, regardless what activities she was outwardly engaged in. Yogis say that even when the body sleeps, there is a continuous awareness of Unity.[12] Sleep, after all, is unconsciousness, and in the seventh and most interior dwelling place, there is no unconsciousness, no darkness at all.

Ramana Maharshi tells us that once we are established in that state in which our mind is 'extinct', we will act 'without effort'. Our decisions, actions, and words come spontaneously, without premeditation, since we are not entertaining a 'thought-process'. We live in the 'eternal present'. Past and future are conditionings of the mind that we have shed. How can we retain a memory of pleasures and pains, successes and failures, when past and future cease to exist for us? Fear, worry, anxiety, guilt, anticipation, desires, all these and more are gone.

OUR HEART 'FLOODS WITH COMPASSION' FOR ALL LIFE

That is indeed a blessed state. As Thich Nhat Hahn explains, it brings forth our deep love for all life: "When your mind is liberated your heart floods with compassion. ...Now you look at yourself and at others with the eyes of compassion, like a saint who hears the cry of every creature in the universe and whose voice is the voice of every person who has seen reality in perfect wholeness."[13] Teresa comments that when we have reached the end of our spiritual journey, we feel a 'particular love' for those who would 'persecute' us.

The 'family' of one who has become 'all-Life' stretches around the whole world. Eknath Easwaran comments:

> It is not that we love our partner or children any less. We love them much more, but now we feel equal love for all. There is nothing sentimental about this. It is thoroughly practical. Every child becomes your child, each creature part of your family; you take care of the planet just as you would your home.[14]

The only motivation of a liberated being is to help others awaken to the unending joy and peace of their true nature. After all, we are conscious as the true life and being of all people, and all creatures. There is no 'other' for us, no barrier of separateness that creates the illusion of two. So we feel the joys and sorrows of others as our very own. Our compassion has no limits. We devote our time and energy to the spiritual development of all those who come within our sphere of influence. Each of us will serve life in a unique way, some more visibly than others. Sometimes a spiritually realized being may even remain hidden to a large degree behind a cloak of normality, to serve and play without attracting attention. And some may even pass from this world unnoticed, having lost all connection to 'name and form'.

Teresa describes how the "fire of love" in us when we are established in union 'enkindles' the soul of others, 'always awakening them. Such service will not be small but very great and very pleasing to the Lord." Liberated beings have the unique power to awaken deep spiritual desire in those who are ready. Wholeness strikes such a deep chord in our being that when we are near one who has become That, our inner being can catch on fire. Once this fire is ignited deep within us, it will gradually grow, and in the end, transfigure us completely.

The consciousness of everyone around a Light-filled person is bound to be lifted, provided they remain open to that influence and do not close themselves off. Such association has the effect of jump-starting them on their own journey. Who can gauge the sphere of influence of one who has realized the Unbounded? Gandhi states unequivocally: "There comes a time when an individual becomes irresistible and his action becomes all-pervasive in its effect. This comes when he reduces himself to zero."[15] Such beings become creators of worlds, worlds of hope, joy, playfulness, and real service. They are never discouraged, and each moment brings a freshness of giving that inspires all.

ಌ

ONCE WE BEGIN OUR JOURNEY, THERE IS NO TURNING BACK

So we have reached journey's end. We have come home, to abide forever in our true nature. Kundalini, the spiritual power deep within our being, has awakened fully and fulfilled its evolutionary purpose. Our core life energy is now 'uncoiled' and stands revealed as pure, infinite Consciousness. Our psyche is unified, and the whole universe is seen in the light of reality, as one indivisible whole. We are that Whole, not a little piece of it, but the Whole itself. We are completely conscious. There is no darkness, nothing hidden within or without us.

It is both a long journey and a great adventure in consciousness to come into the full realization of that which we truly are. It will require much of us, perhaps more than we can imagine. At first we can hardly guess what our real potential is. We have to grow into that. Once kundalini is activated, once that spark of fire burns deep within us, we cannot turn back. The depth of our desire will keep us moving forward through thick and thin, for only true wholeness and true peace will satisfy us.

Chapter 12

Conclusion: Walking on Our Path

"It's hard to be responsible for our own progress. We always seek for someone to carry us and put us on some higher level. We have to understand that our progress is based on our own efforts."
  BABA HARI DASS, IN *Astanga Yoga Primer*

'SATURATING' OUR MIND WITH SPIRITUAL IDEAS AND FEELINGS

The laws of spiritual development must be discovered and proven over and over again, each of us in our own experience. We have no choice but to become journeyers and explorers in the realms of consciousness if we want to understand what spirituality really is. In digging for the treasures of insight, wisdom, and inspiration that are concealed in Teresa's discussion of the seven dwelling places of the interior castle, and in attempting to understand the symbolism of kundalini yoga, each of us must depend, finally, upon our own willingness to walk the path that they map out for us.

Through reading and study we can familiarize ourselves with the nature of the territory that these 'maps' describe. Men and women of true realization often write to inspire and teach, and their words carry a great power to awaken and guide us. Daily spiritual reading is almost a 'must' during the first half of our journey. We have to sustain our inspiration and resolve somehow, and that is one way we can do it. The more we 'saturate' our mind in spiritual ideas and feelings, the more they take root in our being.

FAITH AND DEVOTION ARE OUR LEGS

My teacher always said that faith and devotion are the legs we use to walk on our path. As we take many little steps to awaken our latent spirituality, gradually we gain a deeper conviction that walking on our spiritual path is our life and our destiny. It is no small thing to know for certain what our life-purpose is and where our path lay. Once we have that deep clarity, we have already reached some unification of our being. Then we can apply ourselves with more energy and focus. When we are fighting a powerful *samskara* or deeply rooted tendency within us, and we feel nearly overwhelmed by the challenge of it all, we can find contentment in knowing that no matter where we are in life, no matter how long it takes, we have only one real destiny: to complete our evolutionary journey, for the benefit of all beings.

When our desire to realize the promise of true peace, wholeness, freedom, and compassion becomes a powerful force active in the very depths of our being, we will begin making significant progress. In the yoga tradition, the energy within us that wakes us up, starts us moving, and propels us past countless obstacles and impediments is called kundalini. A dormant spark, hidden away deep in our being, sleeping far from sight, sooner or later it must be ignited, for it is the evolutionary energy of all consciousness, which seeks, as Jung said, to grow out of its limited, unconscious condition and discover its natural wholeness, purity, and indivisibility.

SPIRITUAL PRACTICE: 'FUEL' FOR THE INNER FIRE

Gradually, as we undertake serious spiritual practice, that deep longing for wholeness sets our inner being on fire. *Sadhana,* or daily spiritual practice, is the fuel that feeds that fire. Without it no heat can be generated, and the profound transformation that is symbolized by the awakening of kundalini will not take place. If we tend the inner fire every day for many years, with real devotion, meeting as best we can the many challenges that come our way, it will slowly begin to transfigure our whole being.

We will come, sooner or later, into a completely unwavering faith in our spiritual practice to keep us moving forward on our path. When our dedication is rock solid, we will persevere through every storm, and we will gradually go deeper and deeper. When we gain a little depth, our meditation becomes the primary daily nourishment for our whole being. In giving ourselves to it more fully, with more energy and devotion, we receive back a source of strength that depends on nothing outside ourselves. It is ours to keep and to build.

☙

ALL TRUE EXPLORERS NEED DARING AND COURAGE

We are always moving forward into the unknown. Most of the time, we cannot see the path very far ahead of us, if at all. And we may not even know where we are. We may need to wade through the 'muck' for long periods before we reach any solid ground. Our mind and its deep universal conditioning of fear, anxiety, separateness, and doubt will almost surely confuse us and surround us in darkness at times.

Like all true explorers, we will need our share of daring and courage. We don't always possess as much of those qualities as we would like to begin with, but they grow, little by little, as we exercise that which we do have. The essential thing is to keep moving forward, to keep our spiritual practice alive and vital and growing. We will surprise ourselves one day with a degree of boldness and courage that we didn't even know we had.

A 'LEAP' INTO THE UNKNOWN

After awhile, we will acquire some measure of inner depth and silence. Perhaps only a little bit at first, but gradually more if we keep giving our best. We can learn to 'rest' in that quietness, that sense of peace. That is most helpful, especially when the battles rage fiercely around us. The challenges we will face grow more formidable as we walk forward on our path. So if we can learn to rest a little in the silence and Mystery, we will draw the nourishment we need to face those challenges. Even a little 'hint' of spiritual peace can really motivate us, for our whole being wants to reach the place, as Teresa says, where that peace is 'unending'.

We learn gradually to set our eyes on the Ideal, which, in truth, is the Real. The more deeply we can become convinced that we are infinite Life, and the whole world is That, hidden beneath the appearance of duality, the more completely will we be motivated to give ourselves to our path. We begin to 'own' our spiritual destiny. That faith and that resolve becomes crucial after awhile. With it, we can gather strength to leave our familiar surroundings and make the leap into the unknown that 'waking up' in the unconscious requires.

That great leap to 'complete consciousness' is ours to make, or not, as the depth of our spiritual desire dictates. We have to 'give' a lot and 'give up' a lot to do it. As Teresa says, there is a price to be paid for Unity and Peace. If we want that, in the end we have to 'up the ante' considerably in life and play all our cards. We cannot hold back. We cannot be 'free' and still cling to anything.

Let each person contemplate the vision given to us by *Interior Castle* and kundalini yoga, which are different maps of the same territory. Let each of us, according to our desire, grow in the spirit of fierce devotion and daring faith that alone enables us little specks of individual consciousness to travel far and deep until we discover and enter into and 'be' the All-Consciousness that pervades and 'is' the whole of creation, our very Life.

Endnotes

Chapter 1:
1. C. G. Jung, *Memories, Dreams, Reflections*, p. 3. With this statement, Jung begins his autobiography. This book offers a fascinating look at the life-work of one of the most influential thinkers and explorers of the modern world.
2. See Eknath Easwaran, *The Dhammapada*, p. 57.

Chapter 2:
1. Haridas Chaudhuri, 'Yoga Psychology' in *Transpersonal Psychologies*, p. 265.
2. Swami Pratyagatmananda, 'Tantra as a Way of Realization' in *Studies on the Tantras*, p. 80.
3. Sir John Woodruffe, *The Serpent Power*, p. 6. This book, first published in 1919, is one of the most thorough and technical commentaries on kundalini yoga that exist. Woodruffe, also known as Arthur Avalon, was a British judge living in Calcutta. He became a serious student of the tradition. The West knew nothing about kundalini yoga until this book became available in the 1920s. It was the basis for Jung's 1932 seminars.
4. Lama Anagarika Govinda, *Foundations of Tibetan Mysticism*, p. 142.
5. See, for example, Anodea Judith, *Eastern Body, Western Mind*.
6. C. G. Jung, *The Psychology of Kundalini Yoga*. This book contains the transcripts of Jung's 1932 kundalini yoga seminars. Since I quote it often, I am not going to cite it and give specific page references each time. The interested reader can read the four seminar transcripts quickly enough.
7. Govinda, *Foundations of Tibetan Mysticism*, pp. 167–168.

Chapter 3:
1. I do not cite individual references from *Interior Castle*. Unless otherwise noted, they are all from the authoritative translations of her works by Kavanaugh and Rodriguez, as are the occasional quotes from *Book of Her Life*, Teresa's autobiographical work written about seven years before *Interior Castle*.

Chapter 4:

1. Emilie Cady, an American 'seer' and spiritual teacher in the 'New Thought' traditions, wrote *Lessons in Truth* in the 1890s.
2. Easwaran, *Conquest of Mind*, p. 8.
3. *ibid.*, p. 8.
4. Swami Hariharananda Aranya, *Yoga Philosophy of Patanjali*, p. 36.
5. Thich Nhat Hahn, *Miracle of Mindfulness*, pp. 60–61.
6. *ibid.*, pp. 35–36.
7. Easwaran, *Like a Thousand Suns*, p. 138.
8. See Chaudhuri, *Philosophy of Meditation*, pp. 44–48; and Easwaran, *Like a Thousand Suns*, pp. 237–238.
9. C. G. Jung, 'The Psychology of Eastern Meditation' in *Psychology and the East*, p. 171.
10. See Heinrich Zimmer, *Philosophies of India*, pp. 294–295.

Chapter 5:

1. Easwaran, *Dialogue with Death*, pp. 23–24.
2. For color plates depicting the chakras, and for very accessible detailed descriptions of them, see Harish Johari, *Chakras*.
3. See David Fideler, *Jesus Christ, Sun of God*, pp. 309–315.
4. Swami Chinmayananda, *Talks on Sankara's Vivekachoodamani*, p. 219.

Chapter 6:

1. Easwaran, *Conquest of Mind*, p. 73.
2. See Easwaran, *Like a Thousand Suns*, p. 27.
3. C. G. Jung, 'Commentary on *The Secret of the Golden Flower*' in *Psychology and the East*, p. 20.
4. See Easwaran, *Like A Thousand Suns*, p. 210.
5. Easwaran, *To Love Is To Know Me*, pp. 351–352.

Chapter 7:

1. C. G. Jung, 'Forward to Suzuki's *Introduction to Zen Buddhism*' in *Psychology and the East*, p. 156.
2. Govinda, *Foundations of Tibetan Mysticism*, pp. 160–161.
3. Mimi Frazer, 'The Path to Reality' in *Vedanta for Modern Man*, p. 242.
4. Shyam Sundar Goswami, *Laya Yoga*, p. 320.

5. Sri Ramana Maharshi, *The Collected Works of Ramana Maharshi*, p. 49.
6. Swami Prabhavananda, *How To Know God*, p. 59.
7. See Easwaran, *To Love Is To Know Me*, pp.178–179, 181–182, and 196.

Chapter 8:
1. See Alain Danielou, *The Myths and Gods of India*, p. 91.
2. Goswami, *Laya Yoga*, p. 144.
3. Zimmer, *Philosophies of India*, pp. 48–49.
4. Easwaran, *To Love Is To Know Me*, p. 433.
5. C. G. Jung, 'Forward to Suzuki's *Introduction to Zen Buddhism*' in *Psychology and the East*, p. 151.
6. Easwaran, *To Love Is To Know Me*, p. 206.
7. Quoted in Easwaran, *Gandhi the Man*, p. 110.
8. C. G. Jung, 'Commentary on *The Secret of the Golden Flower*' in *Psychology and the East*, pp. 39–40.
9. Swami Ashokananda, *Meditation, Ecstasy, and Illumination*, p. 244.

Chapter 9:
1. Goswami, *Laya Yoga*, p. 148.
2. See Easwaran, *To Love Is To Know Me*, p. 54 and pp. 367–368.
3. Woodruffe, *The Serpent Power*, p. 169.
4. Easwaran, *Dialogue with Death*, p. 120.
5. Aranya, *Yoga Philosophy of Patanjali*, p. 24.
6. Easwaran, *Like a Thousand Suns*, p. 273.
7. Easwaran, *Dialogue with Death*, p. 162.
8. Goswami, *Laya Yoga*, p. 57.
9. Easwaran, *Dialogue with Death*, p. 211.
10. Ashokananda, *Meditation, Ecstasy, and Illumination*, p. 241.
11. Easwaran, *Dialogue with Death*, p. 188.
12. Easwaran, *To Love Is To Know Me*, p. 111.
13. Ashokananda, *Meditation, Ecstasy, and Illumination*, pp. 235–236.
14. See Aranya, *Yoga Philosophy of Patanjali*, p. 131.

Chapter 10:
1. Chaudhuri, *Philosophy of Meditation*, p. 77.
2. See Johari, *Chakras*, pp. 20–28, for a detailed description of the *nadis*.

3. See Easwaran, *To Love Is To Know Me*, p. 55–56.
4. Easwaran, *Like a Thousand Suns*, p. 130.
5. Swami Rama, *Inspired thoughts of Swami Rama*, p. 219.
6. Easwaran, *To Love Is To Know Me*, p. 469.
7. Aranya, *Yoga Philosophy of Patanjali*, p. 313.
8. Swami Vivekananda, *Raja Yoga*, p. 94.
9. Goswami, *Laya Yoga*, p. 25.
10. Aranya, *Yoga Philosophy of Patanjali*, p. 104.

Chapter 11:
1. See Johari, *Chakras*, p. 87.
2. Easwaran, *Like a Thousand Suns*, p. 138.
3. See Johari, *Chakras*, pp. 81–85.
4. Easwaran, *Dialogue with Death*, p. 173.
5. Easwaran, *To Love Is To Know Me*, p. 448.
6. Easwaran, *Conquest of Mind*, p. 127.
7. See Aranya, *Yoga Philosophy of India*, pp. 397–398.
8. See Vivekananda, *Raja Yoga*, pp. 264–265.
9. Chinmayananda, *Talks on Sankara's Vivekachoodamani*, p. 384.
10. Easwaran, *Dialogue with Death*, p. 177.
11. See Prabhavananda, *How To Know God*, p. 16 and p. 32.
12. See Easwaran, *To Love Is To Know Me*, p. 172.
13. Thich Nhat Hahn, *Miracle of Mindfulness*, pp. 58–59.
14. Easwaran, *Dialogue with Death*, p. 208.
15. Quoted in Easwaran, *Gandhi the Man*, p. 114.

Bibliography

Aranya, S. H. *Yoga Philosophy of Patanjali*. Albany, NY: State University of New York Press, 1983.
Ashokananda, S. *Meditation, Ecstasy, and Illumination*. Calcutta: Advaita Ashrama, 1990.
Chaudhuri, H. "Yoga Psychology." *Transpersonal Psychologies*. Tart, C. (ed). New York: Harper & Row, 1975.
Chaudhuri, H. *Philosophy of Meditation*. New York: Philosophical Library, 1965.
Chinmayananda, S. *Talks on Sankara's Vivekachoodamani*. Bombay: Central Chinmaya Mission Trust, 1976.
Danielou, A. *The Myths and Gods of India*. Rochester, VT: Inner Traditions International, 1985.
Easwaran, E. *Gandhi the Man*. Petaluma, CA: Nilgiri Press, 1978.
The End of Sorrow: Vol. 1. The Bhagavad Gita for Daily Living. Petaluma, CA: Nilgiri Press, 1975.
Like a Thousand Suns: Vol. 2. The Bhagavad Gita for Daily Living. Petaluma, CA: Nilgiri Press, 1979.
Dialogue with death. Petaluma, CA: Nilgiri Press, 1981.
To Love Is To Know Me: Vol. 3. The Bhagavad Gita for Daily Living. Petaluma, CA: Nilgiri Press, 1984.
(ed. and trans.) *The Dhammapada*. Petaluma, CA: Nilgiri Press, 1985.
Conquest of Mind. Petaluma, CA: Nilgiri Press, 1988.
Fideler, D. *Jesus Christ, Sun of God*. Wheaton, IL: The Theosophical Publishing House, 1993.
Frazer, M. "The Path to Reality." *Vedanta for Modern Man*. Isherwood, C. (ed.) New York: Mentor, 1972.
Goswami, S.S. *Laya Yoga*. Rochester, VT: Inner Traditions, 1999.
Govinda, L. A. *Foundations of Tibetan Mysticism*. York Beach, ME: Samuel Weiser, 1969.
Johari, H. *Chakras*. Rochester, VT: Inner Traditions, 1987.
Judith, A. *Eastern body, Western mind*. Berkeley, CA: Ten Speed Press, 1997.
Jung, C. G. "Commentary on *The Secret of the Golden Flower*." *Psychology and the East*. Hull, R. F. C. (trans.) Bollingen Series XX, Princeton, NJ: Princeton University Press, 1978.

"Forward to Suzuki's *Introduction to Zen Buddhism*." *Psychology and the East*. Hull, R. F. C. (trans.) Bollingen Series XX, Princeton, NJ: Princeton University Press, 1978.

"The Psychology of Eastern Meditation." *Psychology and the East*. Hull, R. F. C. (trans.) Bollingen Series XX, Princeton, NJ: Princeton University Press, 1978.

Memories, Dreams, Reflections. New York: Random House, 1965.

The Psychology of Kundalini Yoga. Shamdasani, S. (ed.) Bollingen Series XCIX, Princeton, NJ: Princeton University Press, 1996.

Lipski, Dr. A. *Life and Teaching of Sri Anandamayi Ma*. Delhi: Motilal Banarsidass, 1977.

M. *The Gospel of Sri Ramakrishna*. New York: Ramakrishna-Vivekananda Center, 1942.

New Jerusalem Bible. New York: Doubleday, 1985.

Plato. *The Republic of Plato*. Cornford, F. M. (trans.) London: Oxford University Press, 1941.

Prabhavananda, S. *How to Know God*. New York: Signet, 1953.

Pratyagatmananda, S. "Philosophy of the Tantras." *Studies on the Tantras*. Calcutta: Ramakrishna Mission Institute of Culture, 1989.

"Tantra as a Way of Realization." *Studies on the Tantras*. Calcutta: Ramakrishna Mission Institute of Culture, 1989.

Rama, S. *Inspired Thoughts of Swami Rama*. Honesdale, PA: Himalayan Institute Press, 1983.

Ramana Maharshi, Sri. *The Collected Works of Ramana Maharshi*. Madras: Sri Ramanasramam, 1979.

Teresa of Avila. *The Interior Castle. The Collected Works of St. Teresa of Avila*, Vol. II. Kavanaugh, K. and Rodriguez, O., (trans.) Washington, D.C.: ICS Publications, 1980.

The Book of Her Life. The Collected Works of St. Teresa of Avila, Vol. I. Kavanaugh, K. and Rodriguez, O., (trans.) Washington, D.C.: ICS Publications, 1976.

Interior Castle. Peers, E. A. (trans.) New York: Doubleday, 1961.

Hahn, T. N. *Miracle of Mindfulness*. Boston: Beacon Press, 1975.

Vivekananda, S. *Raja Yoga*. Calcutta: Advaita Ashrama, 1992.

Woodruffe, Sir J. *The Serpent Power*. New York: Dover, 1974.

Zimmer, H. *Philosophies of India*. New York: Meridian Books, 1956.

Sanskrit Glossary

Note: This is a glossary of Sanskrit terms as they are used in this book. In the interest of simplicity, I have omitted all diacritical marks.

ahamkara: the ego or 'I-maker' function in individual consciousness by which 'I' becomes identified with body, mind, world, and life experiences.

ajna: authority, command, power. The sixth chakra located in the area between the eyebrows.

akasha: ether, space. The most subtle and least manifest realm of material/mental existence.

amrita: nectar. The ambrosial liqueur that symbolizes the flow of true spiritual peace and joy in the fully awakened consciousness.

anahata: unstruck. Refers to a subtle interior sound that may be heard in deep meditation. The name of the fourth, or heart chakra.

bhakti: spiritual devotion

bindu: point. In meditation, complete concentration on a single point.

chakra: wheel. In kundalini yoga, one of the seven centers of energy and consciousness pictured as aligned along the spinal column.

cittavritti: fluctuation of the mind. Any thought, feeling, sensation, perception, etc.

dharana: concentration. A deep state of meditation in which the mind fixes itself on a single object of concentration.

dharma: way or path consistent with universal spiritual law

dharma-megha: cloud of virtue. Refers to a deep state of meditative absorption that ensues after all attachments are forsaken, including supernormal knowledge and powers.

dhyana: a deeper state of meditation than *dharana* in which the mind flows uninterruptedly, without even small breaks, toward the object of concentration *guna*: quality. The three primary qualities that combine to create the world of matter and mind: *sattva* or purity, sentience; *rajas* or energy, activity; *tamas* or inertia, unconsciousness.

hamsa: mythical wild swan, symbolizing the freedom of true self-realization

ida: one of the primary *nadi(s)* or energy channels in the human body and psyche. *Ida* is the carrier of female, lunar energies. *Pingala* is the carrier of male, solar energies.

jivan mukta: free while living. Refers to one who, through spiritual development, has awakened or become conscious as the infinite, eternal Reality underlying all existence.

karma: action. The fruit of our past actions, including even mental actions or thoughts.

klesha: affliction. Refers to 5 fundamental conditioned tendencies in our psyche: nescience or unconsciousness of our true nature, the ego function, attraction, aversion, fear of death.

kundalini: the evolutionary energy deep within our psyche that propels us on a path of spiritual development. Symbolized by a serpent coiled at the base of the spine in the root chakra.

laya yoga: the spiritual path of dissolving our mind. Another name for kundalini yoga.

lingam: a phallic symbol associated with the god Shiva and symbolizing spiritual reality as pure, uncreated, absolute

mahat: universal mind, associated with the sixth chakra

makara: a mythical sea monster, associated with the second chakra

mandala: circle. A sacred geometric pattern based on a circle, and often incorporating a square as well. Jung treated them as symbols of psychic wholeness.

manipura: city of jewels. The name of the third chakra.

maya: illusion. The universal mind conditioning present in all created beings, causing us to be unconscious of our spiritual nature and conscious only of the world of name and form.

mayashakti: the creative, projecting energy of consciousness that generates the stream of consciousness and dazzles us with the myriad world of appearances. Another name for kundalini in her sleeping, 'world-bewilderer' state.

muladhara: root support. The name of the lowest or first chakra.

nadi: energy channel with the body and psyche

namarupa: name and form. Refers to the world as perceived by our senses and mind.

niralambapuri: dwelling place without support. Refers to the crown chakra or final stage of spiritual development.

nirodha: cessation, also inhibition

nirvana: the state of having been blown out or extinguished. Refers to the final goal of spiritual development, when we become established in the 'peace that passeth all understanding'.

prana: the fundamental energy within creation. In human beings, the life-force that animates both body and mind.

pratyahara: withdrawal of the mind from fascination with objects perceived by the senses. A process of interiorizing our consciousness that is a prerequisite of deep meditation.

sabdabrahman: pure spiritual reality manifesting as sound, ideation, language

sadhana: daily spiritual practice as part of a committed path of development

sahasrara: thousand-petalled. The name of the crown or uppermost chakra.

samadhi: deep meditative absorption in which the duality of subject and object is transcended

samskara: a strong conditioned tendency or pattern that motivates us unconsciously

shakti: the divine as the creative power of the universe

siddhi: a supernormal power. May be possible to acquire in the latter stages of spiritual development.

sunya: empty, void. Refers to the final stage of spiritual practice when the mind is dissolved and spiritual reality remains alone, in its own pure nature.

sushumna: the secret channel that connects the chakras through which kundalini moves upward when aroused and awakened. Psychologically, the pathway from the surface of our mind to the spiritual essence hidden in the most interior depth of our being.

svadhisthana: dwelling place of the self. The name of the second chakra.

svayambhu: self-born, self-existent, not dependent on anything else. The nature of pure spirit.

ଔ

tapas: heat. Psychic heat generated by personal sacrifice for the sake of spiritual development.

tattva: a fundamental realm within the structure of psyche and cosmos. There are 5 realms that correspond with the lower five chakras.

tattvatita: transcending all the realms of matter/mind creation. An advanced state of spiritual development associated with the sixth chakra.

tejas: brilliance, radiance

vayu: air, wind. The Vedic god of wind.

vishuddha: pure. The name of the fifth chakra.

vritti: fluctuation of the mind. Any movement or function of the mind, however subtle.

yoga: union, or wholeness of being that comes when the mind process is fully controlled and we become conscious in the spiritual depth of our being. Also the path that leads to this state.

yoni: female sexual organ symbolizing creation, nature, the manifest universe.

Index

ahamkara, 85, 168
ajna chakra, 179–184, 188–189
anahata chakra, 141–148
akasha, 162
archetypes, 35, 165–166
awakening, 12, 40
Baba Hari Dass, 31, 69, 150, 215
Bhagavad Gita, 134, 156
bindu, 195
Cady, Emilie, 222
chakras,
    and the subtle body, 19
    as consciousness potentials, 15
chakra system,
    and personality development, 18–19
    as a developmental model, 8, 17
    as a map of the psyche, 18, 22–23, 25, 51
    polar nature of, 22–23, 25
    symbolic nature of, 6, 17, 21, 26
Chaudhuri, Haridas, 15, 64, 180
Churning of the Milky Ocean, myth of, 63–64, 184
complete consciousness, 7, 46–47, 55, 200, 202–204, 213
conscious—unconscious polarity, 8, 11, 22, 49, 81, 208
death, 201
depth psychology, 1–2, 22, 29, 49
    and imagery of *Interior Castle*, 35, 40
    language of, 8
    relationship to Kundalini yoga, 8, 22
devil(s), 41, 93, 104, 107–108
dharana— dhyana—samadhi, 170–171

'dwelling places' within the castle of the psyche, 36–40
Easwaran, Eknath, 56, 62, 108, 117, 121, 134, 169, 173, 175, 184, 198, 200, 201, 205, 211
ego, 10–11, 26, 85, 104, 136, 168, 210
    dissolution of, 207
Gandhi, Mahatma, 156, 212
God, 108
    idea of, 80, 187–188
    union with, 5, 34, 190, 202–204
Goswami, Shyam Sundar, 162, 170
gunas, 152–153
hamsa bird, 144–145
higher knowledge, 176–178
Hymn of the Pearl, 88–89
humility, 42, 92–93
individuation, 8–9, 137–138, 147
Interior Castle, 5–6, 34
    theme of, 37, 203
    dwelling places within, 36–40, 102
    religious language of, 40–41, 107
John-of-the-Cross, 176
Jung, C. G., 1, 8, 221
    and 1932 Kundalini yoga seminars, 21–22, 78
    eloquence on 'root' chakra, 76–80
    on individuation, 5, 9, 115, 137, 157
    on meditation, 66–67, 153–154
    on non-duality, 200
    on the psychology of the God-idea, 187–188
    on the unconscious, 22
karma, law of, 113–114
kleshas, 67, 178

kundalini,
    and therapy, 18–19
    arousal of, 20, 90, 126, 154
    ascent of, 17, 20
    as world-bewilderer, 75
    serpent, symbolism of, 27, 30, 74, 98
Kundalini yoga, 6, 16
    relationship to *Interior Castle*, 50
Lama Govinda, 30, 126
manipura chakra, 120–124, 126, 142, 147
meditation, 45–46, 53–69, 90–91, 94, 110, 131–132, 135, 140, 153, 158, 166, 170–171
mind process, dissolution of, 207–210
muladhara chakra, 22, 72–80, 85, 91, 97, 99, 100, 124
non-attachment, 112–113, 156–157, 208
non-ego, 10–11, 136, 188
Plato's cave analogy, 86–87
prana, 19, 72, 126, 154
prayer, 44–45, 59, 91, 158
projection, 11, 55, 76, 80, 82
    withdrawal of, 55, 106, 110–112, 132–134, 155, 167, 208
psyche, 9, 34–35
recollection, 106, 109–110, 135, 155
sahasrara chakra, 22, 29, 197–198, 200
samskaras, 125, 132, 216
self-knowledge, 42, 92–93
sexual energy, 115–118
Sir John Woodruffe, 30, 164

'spiritual delights', 148–149, 159
spiritual marriage, 48–49, 172, 192, 202–204
spiritual practice, 57, 90, 103, 109–111, 147, 217
spiritual psychology, 2, 12–13, 34
Sri Anandamayi Ma, 97
Sri Ramana Maharshi, 135–136, 210
subtle body, yoga theory of, 19
sushumna, 20, 74, 98, 181–182
svadhisthana chakra, 98–100, 113, 116–117
Swami Ashokananda, 158
Swami Vivekananda, 184, 193
tattva, 25, 121, 182
Teresa of Avila, 1, 6, 34
Thich Nhat Hahn, 58, 61, 179, 211
The Psychology of Kundalini Yoga, 8
The Secret of the Golden Flower, 157
The Serpent Power, 30, 164, 221
transformation of consciousness, 7, 22, 39
unconscious conditioning, 27–31, 37, 47, 77–78, 80, 84, 94, 101, 104–107, 125, 175
    freedom from, 198–199
unification of desires, 57, 130–131, 139, 151, 196
universal unconscious, 23, 31, 178, 183
vishuddha chakra, 161–166
wholeness, 8–9, 35, 49–50, 88–89, 126, 135, 217
Yoga Sutras, 54, 57, 193, 209
Zimmer, Heinrich, 144